Generative AI for Social Media Marketing

*Tools and Techniques to Build Profitable
Digital Campaigns for Online Business*

By
Samy Boustany

TABLE OF CONTENTS

INTRODUCTION

ARTIFICIAL INTELLIGENCE

A rtificial intelligence (AI) is a field that has captured the imagination of scientists, engineers and enthusiasts of technology from around the world. The scientists' goal is to create machines that can mimic human abilities, such as logical thinking, reasoning, problem-solving and learning. The study of artificial intelligence is a multidisciplinary field that combines concepts and methods from mathematics, statistics, cognitive psychology, neuroscience, and computer science. The goal of AI is to develop systems that can process information in a similar way that humans do. To achieve this goal, the tool at our disposal is machine learning: by which using algorithms and mathematical models we can enable machines to "learn" from data and improve their performance over time. There are several types of machine learning, but one of the most common is what is known as supervised learning.

In this approach, a machine learning model is trained on a matching set of input data (features) and output data (labels). The goal is to develop a model that can generalize the relationship between inputs and outputs and make accurate predictions on new data. A simple example of supervised learning is a model that has to recognize whether a picture contains a cat or a dog. During the training phase, the model is given for analysis, a set of pictures of cats and dogs, accompanied by their correct labels. Through learning, the model learns to identify the distinguishing features between the two animals and can then make correct predictions on new pictures. In addition to supervised learning, there are also other machine learning approaches such as unsupervised learning and reinforcement learning. Unsupervised learning focuses on identifying patterns and structures in the data without the aid of explicit labels. This can be useful for data segmentation, dimensionality reduction or cluster discovery. Reinforcement learning, on the other hand, involves an agent making decisions in a dynamic environment by interacting with it. The agent receives "reinforcement signals" based on its actions, and its goal is to maximize a reward function in the long run. This approach is often used in applications such as games, robotics, and resource management. The field of application of artificial intelligence and machine learning is vast and undoubtedly expanding. Today, we find AI in many aspects of our daily lives, although we often do not realize it. Search engines such as Google use machine learning algorithms to provide relevant and personalized search results. Streaming services such as Netflix use AI to recommend content based on our tastes and preferences. Autonomous cars rely on AI to drive safely and intelligently. In addition, AI is widely used in medicine, finance, cybersecurity, natural language processing and many other areas. Unfortunately, artificial intelligence, however, presents challenges and ethical issues as well. A major concern is the ethics of AI and the impact it may have on society. AI along with development on robotics and automation could lead to job losses in many industries, raising questions about the equitable redistribution of resources. What we risk is an increase in inequality among the strata of society with the increase in difficulties related to the creation of new opportunities. AI can be influenced by the data with which it is trained and could thus perpetuate biases and discrimination present in society, going on to amplify them and eventually make them a standard. To address these challenges, it is important to develop a sound ethical framework for the use of AI. This involves transparency in AI decisions, accountability of developers and users, and consideration of possible social and economic impacts. Research and studies need to be done not only with regard to technology, but also with regard to ethics and law in order to be able to create appropriate rules and legislation.

2

AI has the potential to transform industries, improve quality of life, and enable breakthrough scientific discoveries. However, it is critical that AI is developed and used ethically, taking into account societal implications and ensuring that its impact is positive for humanity as a whole. Artificial intelligence (AI) has captured the collective imagination and rapidly integrated itself into almost every aspect of our lives. From apps on our smartphones to the complex systems powering the global economy, AI has become an unstoppable force, pushing humanity to new horizons. Artificial intelligence is often considered the edge of technology, a field in which science seeks to replicate the cognitive capabilities of humans in a computer. But unlike popular depictions in movies, where androids can walk, talk and even express emotions like humans, the true essence of AI is much less anthropomorphic and much more focused on specific tasks and processes.

ORIGINS OF THE TERM

The word "artificial" is clear: it refers to something man-made, not natural. "Intelligence," however, is a more elusive concept. In general, intelligence can be defined as the ability to perceive, understand, reason and respond to one's surroundings. When we talk about "artificial intelligence," we are essentially referring to systems designed to replicate these cognitive capabilities.

Definition of Artificial Intelligence

When we talk about "artificial intelligence," what exactly do we mean? AI refers to the ability of a system to perform tasks that would typically require human intelligence. These can include tasks such as speech recognition, decision making, translation between languages, and even artistic creation. AI is not a new concept. Already in ancient myths and legends, the idea of animated statues or mechanical objects that could think and act like human beings was a popular subject. However, modern AI has little to do with these myths and much more to do with mathematics, computer science and the vast amount of data available.

A brief history of AI

The roots of artificial intelligence go back to the 20th century. The early vision of AI was led by pioneers such as Alan Turing, whose famous "Turing test" proposed a criterion for determining whether a machine could be considered "intelligent." Since then, AI has gone through periods of intense enthusiasm followed by decades of disappointment, commonly known as "AI winters." But the latest decade has seen an explosion in AI interest and applications. The reason? Advances in machine learning, particularly in a subset called "deep learning," and the availability of huge amounts of online data.

Fundamental applications of AI

The applications of AI are vast and growing every day. In healthcare, AI helps doctors diagnose diseases and predict outcomes for patients. In the financial sector, it is used to analyze trading patterns and prevent fraud. And in the transportation sector, AI is fueling the race toward fully autonomous vehicles. But perhaps one of the areas most influenced by AI is marketing. With the advent of big data, companies now have access to an unprecedented amount of information about their customers. And AI is becoming the key tool for analyzing and acting on this data. The term "artificial intelligence" may conjure up images of humanoid robots or omniscient supercomputers, but the reality is much more complex and multifaceted. AI refers to the simulation of human intelligence processes by machine systems, particularly computer systems. These processes include learning (the acquisition of information and rules for using information), reasoning (the use of rules to reach approximate or definite conclusions) and self-correction. Unlike standard programming, where a programmer sets specific rules for each possible output, in many AI applications, the machine is programmed to learn from data and experiences and automatically improve its performance over time. There are various approaches and techniques within AI, such as machine learning (where machines learn from data), deep learning (which uses complex neural networks to analyze various data factors), natural language processing and robotics, just to name a few.

Artificial Intelligence Pioneers

Alan Turing: Known as the father of theoretical computer science, Turing proposed the "Turing Test" in 1950 as a criterion for determining whether a machine can be considered "intelligent". His idea was simple: if a human interrogator cannot distinguish between answers given by a computer and those given by a human during a conversation, then the machine can be considered "intelligent."

John McCarthy: Often referred to as the father of AI, McCarthy coined the term "artificial intelligence" in 1955. He also initiated the first AI research program at the Massachusetts Institute of Technology (MIT) and later at Stanford University.

Marvin Minsky: Co-founder of MIT's Artificial Intelligence Laboratory, Minsky has been a major contributor to the theory and development of AI. He has written numerous books on the subject and has influenced the direction and perception of AI for decades.

Rosa Rao: Less well known than other pioneers, Rao played a crucial role in adapting AI to engineering applications and contributed to bridges between AI theory and practical application.

Claude Shannon: Known as the father of information theory, Shannon has had an enormous impact on computer science and, consequently, on AI. His work established the foundation for many of the techniques used in modern AI.

These individuals are just a few of the many who laid the foundation for AI as we know it today. Each of them has made unique and significant contributions to the theory, practice and development of artificial intelligence. 'Artificial intelligence (AI) has achieved unprecedented levels of development and application in recent decades, and its future looks even more promising.

INTRODUCTION TO SOCIAL

MEDIA MARKETING

In today's digital age, companies are having to navigate an increasingly complex and interconnected media landscape. With the advent of social media platforms such as Facebook, Twitter, Instagram and LinkedIn, the way companies interact with their customers has changed dramatically. Social media has become the new battleground for consumer attention, and Social Media Marketing (SMM) has become an essential part of any company's marketing strategy.

Definition of Social Media Marketing

Social Media Marketing is the use of social media platforms and websites to promote a product or service. However, social media marketing activities go far beyond simple promotion. Including other activities such as interacting with audiences by sharing content, comments and reviews, creating targeted advertising content, and monitoring and analyzing interactions and results.

The Importance of Social Media Marketing

Increased Visibility: A social media presence increases a company's visibility. With nearly 4 billion active users on social media worldwide, it is a channel that cannot be ignored.

Customer Interaction: Social media offers companies the opportunity to interact directly with their customers. This allows them not only to build stronger relationships, but also to receive immediate feedback on products and services.

Targeted Targeting: Social media platforms offer advanced advertising targeting tools that enable companies to reach their target audiences accurately.

Reduced Costs: Compared to other forms of advertising, social media marketing is relatively inexpensive. Many of the social media allow people to create and share content for free, and even paid advertising campaigns are often cheaper than other channels.

SEO improvement: Social media interaction can have a positive impact on search engine rankings. Sharing content on social media can increase traffic to the website, thereby improving its ranking in search results.

Case Study: Starbucks

Starbucks is an excellent example of a company that has effectively harnessed the power of social media. They used various social media platforms to interact with their customers and promote their products. For example, they launched campaigns such as #RedCupContest on Instagram, where they asked customers to share photos of their holiday drinks in a red Starbucks cup for a chance to win a gift card. This campaign not only increased interaction with the brand, but also created a large amount of user-generated content that helped promote Starbucks during the holiday season.

Effective Social Media Marketing Strategies

It is not enough to have a presence on social media, it is essential to have a well-planned and implemented strategy. Here are some successful strategies that companies can adopt:

Goal Setting: First of all, it is necessary to define the goals of Social Media Marketing. These may include increasing brand visibility, acquiring new customers, improving relationships with existing customers, or increasing website traffic.

Knowing the Audience: Understanding your target audience is critical to the success of any marketing campaign. This includes knowing their preferences, their online behaviors, and which social media platforms they use most frequently.

Creation of Quality Content: Content is the king of social media. Creating interesting, informative, and engaging content is essential to attracting and keeping the attention of your audience.

Use of Paid Advertising: Although it is possible to reach a significant audience through sharing free content, paid advertising can help reach a larger and more targeted audience.

Monitoring and Analysis: It is critical to regularly monitor the effectiveness of social media marketing campaigns. This includes analyzing the number of interactions, reach, website traffic and return on investment (ROI).

Case Study: Airbnb

Airbnb is another example of a company that has effectively used social media marketing to promote its brand and services. Using a combination of engaging visual content, sharing campaigns, and collaborations with influencers, Airbnb has managed to build a strong and engaged online community. One notable example is their #LiveThere campaign, launched on Instagram. In this campaign, they asked their followers to share photos of their travel experiences using the hashtag #LiveThere. Not only did this campaign generate a great deal of user- generated content, but it also promoted the idea of traveling as a local, which is at the core of Airbnb's message.

Social Media Marketing Challenges

Despite the many benefits of Social Media Marketing, there are also several challenges that companies face, including:

Information overload: With the vast amount of content shared every day on social media, it is easy for marketing messages to get lost in the crowd.

Changes in Trends and Platforms: Social media trends change rapidly, and what is popular today may not be popular tomorrow. Likewise, social media platforms are constantly evolving, updating their algorithms and features.

Reputation Risks: Social media is a double-edged sword. While they can help build a company's reputation, they can also help damage it. A negative comment or review can spread quickly and have a lasting impact on public perception.

Resources Required: Creating and managing effective social media marketing campaigns takes time and resources. This includes creating content, interacting with audiences, and monitoring and analyzing performance.

Best Practices for Social Media Marketing

Despite the challenges, there are some best practices that can help companies and users themselves maximize the effectiveness of their social media marketing campaigns:

Define a Clear Strategy: This includes defining the goals, identifying the target audience, selecting the most appropriate social media platforms, and planning the type of content to share (it is not important how we define it, we can also simply jot it down on a piece of paper, but it is critical to keep our strategy clear)

Being Authentic: Consumers value authenticity and are more likely to interact with brands that show their human side.

Use Captivating Visual Content: Visual content, such as images and videos, tend to generate more interactions on social media than text-only content.

Interacting with the Public: Responding to comments, sharing user-generated content, and participating in conversations are all ways to build strong relationships with your audience.

Monitor and Adapt: It is important to regularly monitor the effectiveness of campaigns and adapt as necessary. This may include adjusting content, advertising targets or platforms used.

From Traditional Advertising to Social Media Marketing

To understand the crucial importance of social media in modern marketing, we must first examine the nature of advertising itself. For decades, companies have relied on traditional advertising methods: television, radio, newspaper and magazine ads. These methods were effective, but they had inherent limitations: it was difficult to measure their real impact, and their reach was determined by the size and geography of the audience.

With the advent of social media, the rules of the game have changed. Platforms such as Facebook, Instagram, Twitter and LinkedIn have offered companies the opportunity to reach a global audience, 24 hours a day, with highly personalized messages. This micro- targeting capability has revolutionized the way companies communicate with their customers.

The Emergence of the Digital Consumer

Another factor that has elevated the importance of social media is the emergence of the "digital consumer." With constant access to online information and reviews, today's consumers are more informed and discerning than ever before. They desire authentic, personalized, real-time interactions with the brands they love. In this context, social media has become an essential platform for building and maintaining relationships with customers. Through posts, videos, stories and real-time interactions, companies can now build an authentic, engaging and responsive online presence.

ARTIFICIAL INTELLIGENCE AND SOCIAL MEDIA: A STRATEGIC MARRIAGE

With the enormous growth of data generated by social media, it has become critical for companies to have tools that can analyze, interpret and act on this data efficiently. This is where artificial intelligence comes in. AI can help companies better understand their customers, predict emerging trends, personalize advertising campaigns and improve operational efficiency. For example, machine learning algorithms can analyze millions of social media posts to identify emerging sentiments or trends about a product or brand. This ability to "listen" to the customer in real time is a huge advantage for companies, enabling them to quickly adapt to market needs and desires.

The Digital Battlefield

So why is social media considered a "battleground" for companies? The answer lies in the competitive nature of the digital landscape. In an age when any company can have an online presence, it is critical to stand out from the crowd. Companies compete not only for visibility, but also for consumer attention, trust and loyalty. In this scenario, those who can best harness the potential of social media and artificial intelligence will have a significant competitive advantage. In conclusion, we cannot underestimate the importance of social media in the modern marketing landscape. With their global reach, ability for personalization, and real-time interaction, social media are truly the new battleground for businesses. And in this battle, artificial intelligence will be a major ally in ensuring success.

The Humanization of Brands and AI.

In an era dominated by digital, a seemingly contradictory trend is emerging: the humanization of brands. Consumers want to interact with brands that show a human side, tell authentic stories, and demonstrate empathy and understanding. Paradoxically, this is where artificial intelligence comes in. Chatbots, for example, have become essential tools for many companies in providing 24/7 customer support. But the most advanced chatbots do not just answer predefined questions; using advanced machine learning and natural language processing techniques, these chatbots can understand the nuances of customer questions, respond contextually and even emulate human emotions. Strategic use of AI on social media can also help companies identify and interact with key influencers in their industry, allowing them to build authentic partnerships that resonate with their audiences. With AI, companies can analyze social media data to determine which influencers resonate most with their target audiences, thus ensuring more fruitful collaborations.

The Role of Data in Social Media Marketing

One of the most overlooked, yet crucial, aspects of social media marketing is data management and analysis. Every interaction, every post shared, every like or comment, generates a significant amount of data that, if analyzed properly, can provide valuable insights. Thanks to AI, companies now have the tools to analyze this data in a deeper and more meaningful way. Artificial intelligence can identify patterns and trends that may not be immediately visible to the human eye. This means that marketing campaigns can be optimized in real time, allowing companies to adapt to changing market dynamics and consumer preferences.

Risks and Ethical Considerations

However, all is not rosy in the world of AI and social media marketing. As the use of AI increases, new risks and ethical considerations are also emerging. Data privacy is a growing concern, with consumers becoming increasingly aware of how their information is used and shared. Companies must be transparent about how they use AI and consumer data, ensuring that personal information is protected and used ethically. Irresponsible or unethical use of AI can severely damage a company's reputation and undermine consumer trust.

Conclusion

Social media, combined with the advanced capabilities of artificial intelligence, offer unprecedented opportunities for companies to connect, interact and build lasting relationships with their customers. However, like any powerful tool, the use of AI in social media marketing must be approached with strategy, awareness and responsibility. In this new digital battlefield, the companies that manage to balance technological innovation with authenticity and ethics will be the ones that emerge as leaders and earn the trust and loyalty of their customers.

CHAPTER 1

ARTIFICIAL INTELLIGENCE IN THE WORLD OF MARKETING

In the ever-changing landscape of social media, artificial intelligence (AI) has become a transformative force, reshaping the way we interact, market and We connect on these platforms. The integration of artificial intelligence into social media marketing is not just a passing trend, but a fundamental shift that is redefining the boundaries of digital engagement and creativity. A few decades ago, social media was in its infancy, with platforms such as Six Degrees at the forefront. Today, artificial intelligence has permeated every aspect of social media, from content creation to user interaction. The shift from basic digital interactions to personalized experiences based on artificial intelligence marks a significant evolution in the history of social media. Platforms like ChatGPT have revolutionized the way we communicate online, enabling natural and empathetic conversations that were once a pipe dream.

ADVANTAGES OF ARTIFICIAL INTELLIGENCE IN SOCIAL MEDIA MARKETING

The ability of artificial intelligence to understand and predict user preferences has enabled more personalized experiences on social media. By analyzing large amounts of data, artificial intelligence algorithms can personalize content, making digital experiences more intuitive and engaging. This personalization goes beyond simple content recommendations and includes AI-based advertising and customer engagement, offering a level of personalization previously unattainable. Generative AI, a subset of artificial intelligence, has become a buzzword on social media. Leverages advanced algorithms to create unique and engaging content, including images, video, and text. Tools such as Lately and Lensa AI exemplify this trend, demonstrating the potential of artificial intelligence in creating diverse and engaging content that resonates with audiences. The impact of artificial intelligence extends to the management of advertising on social media platforms. With artificial intelligence-based tools, marketers can optimize targeting, content and ad budgets in real time. This feature ensures more effective campaigns, higher engagement rates and better ROI for brands. In the future, the role of artificial intelligence in social media is expected to increase exponentially. From improving content creation to simplifying ad management and enhancing brands' campaigns, artificial intelligence is poised to change the way brands interact with their audiences on social media. However, this progress comes with a caveat: the need to balance the capabilities of artificial intelligence with considerations ethics and maintain a human touch in digital interactions.

Improve customer intelligence and targeting in social media marketing with artificial intelligence

In the dynamic world of social media marketing, artificial intelligence (AI) has been a turning point, especially in improving customer information and targeting. This technological advance is not just a tool, but a revolution in understanding and connecting with the public in ways previously unimaginable. Imagine having a crystal ball that tells you exactly what your audience wants, likes and needs. Artificial intelligence in social media marketing is practically that crystal ball. With about 4.26 billion active users on social media, the potential for tapping into their interests is enormous. Artificial intelligence algorithms deeply analyze users' behavior, preferences and interactions, providing valuable information to marketers. This data-driven approach enables brands to understand their audiences at a granular level, tailoring their strategies to meet specific needs and preferences. Personalization is the foundation of effective social media marketing, and artificial intelligence is its architect. By analyzing large amounts of data, artificial intelligence helps create detailed customer segments based on behavior, demographics and more. This segmentation allows you to create highly targeted content and ads, leading to more meaningful interactions and higher conversion rates. It's like having a conversation personalized with each segment of your audience, making them feel seen and heard. Artificial intelligence not only understands audiences but also extends the possibilities of optimizing advertising campaigns. Artificial intelligence-based tools can change targeting settings, budgets, and bidding strategies in real time, ensuring that your message reaches the right people at the right time. This level of optimization means that the marketing budget is used more effectively, maximizing ROI. In the future, the role of artificial intelligence in improving customer information and targeting in social media marketing will increase. Technology is evolving rapidly, and with it, the opportunities for marketers to connect with their audiences in increasingly meaningful ways. Applying artificial intelligence in social media marketing is not just about the cutting edge; it is also about creating a deeper, more personalized connection with your audience, leading to long-term relationships and loyalty. Artificial intelligence in social media marketing is changing the way brands understand and engage their audiences. By providing unprecedented insights and targeting capabilities, artificial intelligence enables marketers to create more impactful, personalized and effective campaigns, ushering in an era where technical marketing numbers are more connected and informative.

AUTOMATION OF MARKETING ACTIVITIES

In the dynamic world of social media marketing, artificial intelligence (AI) is a breath of fresh air, especially when i t comes to automating marketing activities. It's no longer just about creating posts or targeting ads; Artificial intelligence is reshaping the way brands interact on major platforms, making each action more efficient and productive. One of the biggest challenges for brands on social media is to consistently produce high-quality content. In this case, artificial intelligence will intervene as a savior. Artificial intelligence-based writing tools, such as ChatGPT, can help generate text for social media posts, easing the burden of brainstorming new ideas. You outline the points, choose the tone, and voila: the tool creates the content for you. Automation ensures that content not only meets normal publishing requirements but also maintains the quality that the audience expects. Artificial intelligence is revolutionizing the management of social media advertising. Using complex algorithms it manages to study user behavior and preferences, enabling intelligent targeting of ads. This means that ads are shown to the people most likely to be interested, making campaigns more effective and marketing efforts more profitable. AI tools for social media can also automatically schedule and publish content at the best times. They analyze when users are most active and when posts get the most attention, ensuring that your content is seen by the most people. This strategic moment increases engagement and reach, making your social media presence stronger. In the visual world of social media, artificial intelligence helps create impactful images, such as customized images and branded videos. Artificial intelligence tools provide features such as automatic background removal, image editing, and image generation from text descriptions. This not only improves the appearance of your posts, but also ensures that they are relevant and impactful. Chatbots, powered by artificial intelligence, are revolutionizing customer service on social networks. They handle routine requests efficiently, allowing you to focus on more strategic tasks. These chatbots provide instant feedback, remember previous interactions, and can even help recommend and sell products, improving the overall customer experience. Artificial intelligence in social media marketing is not only a technological advance but also a strategic partner that helps automate and optimize various aspects of marketing. From content creation to ad management, from scheduling to customer service, artificial intelligence is making social media marketing smarter, more personalized and more effective. We live in exciting times when artificial intelligence is opening up new ways to connect with audiences online, transforming social media marketing into a more effective and impactful approach.

IMPROVING CUSTOMER ENGAGEMENT

In the digital age, companies are constantly looking for innovative ways to improve customer engagement because of it, and artificial intelligence (AI) is at the forefront of this revolution. Artificial intelligence in marketing and customer engagement is not just a futuristic concept but a current reality that is reshaping the way companies interact with customers, providing them with personalized experiences, a humanization that was previously possible only in dreams. AI's ability to analyze customer data and provide personalized recommendations represents a turning point in marketing. It enables companies to create content that deeply resonates with audiences, leading to higher engagement rates. Imagine a world in which every piece of content you see seems to be created specifically for you. This is the power of artificial intelligence-based personalization in social media marketing. Chatbots, through natural language processing (NLP) and machine learning, are redefining customer service. They provide quick and accurate responses to customer inquiries around the clock, significantly improving response time and overall customer satisfaction. The constant availability and effectiveness of chatbots makes customers feel valued and heard at all times of the day. The predictive analytics capabilities of artificial intelligence enable companies to predict customer behavior and future trends. This prediction enables marketers to proactively adjust their strategies, ensuring that customer engagement is not only reactive but also predictive. By understanding what customers want in the future, companies can create marketing campaigns that are one step ahead. With the advent of voice assistants such as Alexa and Siri, optimizing content for voice search has become necessary. Artificial intelligence helps companies understand how people use voice search and create content that meets this growing trend. Alignment with customer habits ensures that businesses remain relevant and accessible in the way customers want. AI's role in monitoring social media channels for brand mentions is invaluable. It enables companies to identify engagement opportunities and respond quickly to customer feedback. This real-time interaction fosters a sense of community and responsiveness, showing customers that their opinions and experiences matter. The use of artificial intelligence in social media marketing is changing customer engagement. From personalization to predictive analytics, chatbots to voice search optimization, artificial intelligence enables companies to connect with customers on a deeper and more meaningful level. As AI technology continues to advance, the potential for even more innovative engagement strategies is limitless and promises a future in which customer interactions will be more personalized, responsive and impactful than ever before.

Artificial intelligence (AI) is changing the social media marketing landscape, especially when it comes to measuring and analyzing marketing performance capability. With the enormous amount of data generated on social media platforms, artificial intelligence is becoming an indispensable tool for companies to understand and improve their marketing strategies. Sentiment analysis is one of the most important applications of artificial intelligence in social network analysis. The technology uses algorithms to sift through social media conversations and determine the emotions behind them. As a result, companies can understand what customers think about their products, services or brands, enabling them to refine their offerings. Imagine being able to assess the mood of your audience and adjust your strategy in real time-that's the power of artificial intelligence-based sentiment analysis. Image recognition based on artificial intelligence is another tool that is revolutionizing social media analytics. The latter can identify objects, people and even emotions in images, helping companies track brand mentions and monitor user-generated content. This technology provides information on how a brand is visually perceived on social media, providing insights beyond text analysis. Predictive analytics is a turning point in social media marketing. Artificial intelligence can analyze customer data to predict future behaviors and trends, enabling companies to tailor their marketing campaigns to improve customer engagement and satisfaction. This proactive approach can lead to increased revenue and a stronger marketing strategy. AI helps companies monitor social media channels for brand mentions, providing opportunities for engagement and responding quickly to customer comments. This constant vigilance ensures that companies stay in touch with their audiences and are always ready to interact, thereby improving customer relations. AI-based testing tools, allow companies to optimize their content by testing different variables such as images, headlines and calls to action. These tools use machine learning algorithms to determine the best performing content, helping to maximize engagement and reach. Artificial intelligence is revolutionizing the way companies measure and analyze social media marketing performance. From sentiment analysis to predictive analytics and content optimization, artificial intelligence provides valuable insights into user behavior and engagement. By leveraging these artificial intelligence-based tools, companies can refine their social media strategies, increase customer satisfaction, and ultimately improve their bottom line. The future of social media marketing lies in harnessing the power of artificial intelligence to create more targeted, effective and engaging campaigns.

AI CHALLENGES AND CONSIDERATIONS FOR SOCIAL MEDIA MARKETING

The intersection of social media and artificial intelligence (AI) has created a dynamic landscape full of tremendous opportunities but also significant challenges. When considering the complexity of this convergence, it is essential to understand the issues that arise when artificial intelligence is applied to social media marketing. Artificial intelligence has enhanced social media platforms with greater capabilities, improving users' marketing experiences and enabling personalized content curation. However, this power comes with challenges, including privacy concerns, algorithmic bias, misinformation, and ethical use of artificial intelligence.

Privacy and data protection

The use of artificial intelligence in social networks requires the management of large amounts of user data, raising concerns about privacy and the risk of misuse of personal information. Striking a balance between personalized experiences and protecting user privacy is essential to maintaining trust.

Algorithmic bias: AI algorithms, developed using large data sets, might unintentionally incorporate bias. This can lead to discriminatory behavior and the amplification of controversial content on social networks. Addressing these biases and ensuring transparency in AI systems is essential for equity and inclusion. Disinformation and inaccurate news: The spread of misinformation and fake news on social media platforms is a growing problem. The AI algorithm has difficulty distinguishing between reliable and unreliable sources, making it difficult to effectively combat fake news.

Ethical use of artificial intelligence

Rapid advances in artificial intelligence raise ethical questions about its use in social media. Issues of consent, liability, and potential manipulation require careful consideration and the establishment of ethical principles. In the future, the intersection of artificial intelligence and social media will likely create transformative developments. Improving user experience, moderating content, and developing sound ethical frameworks will promote responsible use of artificial intelligence. Collaboration among platforms, researchers, policy makers, and users will be essential to address the challenges posed by artificial intelligence in social media. Although the integration of artificial intelligence into social media marketing offers significant benefits, it also poses formidable challenges. Thoughtful management of these challenges is essential to unlocking the transformative potential of artificial intelligence while ensuring a secure, inclusive and ethical digital landscape.

ETHICAL AND PRIVACY ISSUES

The integration of artificial intelligence (AI) into social media marketing has opened up a world of possibilities, but it also raises significant ethical and privacy concerns. As artificial intelligence continues to develop and become more ingrained in our digital interactions, it is essential to understand and solve these problems. AI ethics encompasses a set of ethical principles and professional practices used to guide the development and outcomes of AI technology. This involves maximizing impact and minimizing risks and consequences. As artificial intelligence becomes increasingly integrated into our lives, ethical considerations will become an important part of digital culture. Companies are increasingly investing in artificial intelligence, but ensuring its responsible use is a challenge. Misuse or disregard for ethical issues may result in damage to brand reputation, product defects, legal action, and legal problems. Understanding the ethical issues that marketers face is essential to developing a plan to mitigate these business risks and protect brands.

Main ethical concerns of marketing professionals

Job security and relocation: The potential for artificial intelligence to replace human jobs is a cause for concern. However, the goal is to use artificial intelligence to save time and effort, allowing humans to focus on more important tasks.

Privacy Concerns: Privacy, data protection, and security are critical. Brands are investing in security to prevent surveillance, hacking, and cyber attacks by implementing best practices in data collection, storage, and analysis.

Algorithmic bias and *discrimination*: Artificial intelligence can be biased against underrepresented subsets of data, leading to discrimination in AI-generated content, facial recognition software, and advertising activities.

Disinformation: AI flaws can lead to inaccuracies and the spread of misinformation, risking a brand crisis and reputational damage.

Intellectual property and copyright issues: the ability of artificial intelligence to use images, likenesses, or intellectual property of people raises issues of copyright infringement and plagiarism.

Steps to maintain AI ethics.

Establish internal ground rules: Establish an AI ethics team to define responsibilities and goals.

Identify and justify the role of AI: Identify AI tasks that require human oversight and ethical policy goals.

Develop a vendor evaluation process: Evaluate AI-compatible tools and establish an ethical risk process.

Maintain transparency: Develop messages and alerts that demonstrate the reliability of AI.

Continue training: Organize internal training on AI ethics for all team members.

Although artificial intelligence offers enormous advantages in social media marketing, it is essential to address the ethical and privacy challenges involved. By understanding these issues and taking proactive measures, companies can harness artificial intelligence responsibly, ensure ethical standards and protect both their brands and their customers.

DEPENDENCE ON QUANTITY AND QUALITY

In artificial intelligence (AI) for social media marketing, the quality and quantity of data play an essential role. As artificial intelligence continues to expand in business it faces a familiar but important challenge: data quality. Organizations are investing heavily in ensuring data quality, which is essential because of the many different ways it can be compromised. From user input errors to system settings and typos in data conversion scripts, many factors can lead to poor data quality. The business environment is constantly changing, and new quality issues can arise at any time, making data quality an ongoing challenge. AI pipelines using traditional data sources depend on high-quality data just like any other analytics pipeline. However, artificial intelligence also uses many new sources and types of data, which poses unique challenges in terms of data quality. For example, in the past, data such as images, text, and video have not been used as much by methods other than artificial intelligence, causing various data quality problems. Data quality for model building: Images are often labeled by humans to build models, but human error in labeling can lead to inaccuracies. Detecting these errors is difficult and often requires manual review. Data quality for model evaluation: Determining whether an image is clear enough for valid analysis or too blurry is not easy. The complexity of the AI model used can also influence this assessment. The analysis of new types of data, such as images, is still in its infancy, and there is no one-size-fits-all solution. Organizations should research and test data quality in the context of artificial intelligence. It is essential to implement data quality best practices today and plan to update them as new solutions emerge. It is essential to monitor the performance of artificial intelligence models to identify patterns related to misclassifications and errors. Data quality is a common problem for artificial intelligence processes and the data that support them. Recognizing this challenge and taking proactive steps to address it is critical to successfully implementing artificial intelligence in social media marketing. As AI technology and data quality processes develop, the effectiveness of AI applications in social media marketing will continue to improve.

The challenges of integrating with existing artificial intelligence systems for social media marketing

The integration of artificial intelligence (AI) into social media marketing is changing the way companies interact with their audiences. Although artificial intelligence offers many benefits, such as greater efficiency, better targeting, and improved customer experience, its integration with existing systems presents many challenges. Integrating artificial intelligence into social media marketing means not only leveraging new technologies, but also integrating them into the existing structure of a company's marketing strategy and systems. This process can be complex and requires in-depth knowledge of the technology and its practical applications. *Technical* expertise: One of the main challenges is the need for technical expertise. Successful implementation of AI depends not only on the technology itself, but also on the ability to integrate it into an organization's marketing strategy. This requires a team of experts in artificial intelligence and its applications, including software engineers, data scientists and marketing experts.

Data quality: artificial intelligence algorithms rely on high-quality data to make informed decisions. Poor data quality can lead to ineffective marketing strategies. Companies must ensure that their data are accurate, up-to-date, and complete to avoid targeting the wrong audience or making the wrong strategic decisions.

Financial considerations: Implementing artificial intelligence in social media marketing can be costly, with high initial investment and ongoing costs. This can be a significant obstacle, especially for small businesses or startups, and makes it difficult to justify the cost of AI technology.

Privacy and security concerns: With artificial intelligence systems collecting and processing increasing amounts of data, the risk of data breaches is also increasing. Keeping customer data safe is essential in today's digital age, where information can spread quickly and easily.

Lack of human touch: Although artificial intelligence can improve the marketing process, it may not fully replicate the personal touch needed to build strong customer relationships. Artificial intelligence technology, despite its advances, still lacks the emotional intelligence needed to truly understand and connect with customers. To realize the benefits of artificial intelligence while minimizing these challenges, companies must take a strategic approach. This involves carefully evaluating costs, benefits, risks and using technology responsibly. By carefully addressing these integration challenges, companies can improve their social media marketing efforts and position themselves for future growth.

MANAGING EXPECTATIONS AND EXPERIENCE

In today's rapidly evolving digital world, managing customer expectations and experiences and sales in social media marketing is increasingly difficult, especially with the integration of artificial intelligence (AI). Consumers want immediacy and personalization, and artificial intelligence, particularly conversational artificial intelligence, plays an important role in meeting these needs. The advent of artificial intelligence and chatbots in social media marketing has increased customer expectations for timely and personalized services. This change has put pressure on companies to manage customer demand effectively and efficiently. However, those who harness the power of artificial intelligence in customer service are likely to see greater customer satisfaction and loyalty. Artificial intelligence in customer service often involves machines designed to respond in human ways. Advanced artificial intelligence can solve complex problems, understand language and even recognize objects and sounds. However, it is crucial to remember that these machines are programmed by humans and operate on the basis of complex algorithms. Conversational AI, is a more advanced form of chatbot, combines conversations and processes to reduce repetitive tasks. This technology plays an important role in areas such as COVID-19 risk assessment, thus minimizing the burden on medical personnel. It can also engage in human-like conversations, providing users with more natural interaction.

Benefits of artificial intelligence in the management customer expectations

Increased communication capabilities: Artificial intelligence improves communication, ensuring fast and seamless interactions. For example, Henkel's "Stain-Bot" can identify more than 2,500 variations of materials and fabrics, providing quick solutions to customers.

Reduced response time: AI works 24/7, answering customer questions in different time zones, significantly reducing response time.

Personalization of the customer experience: Artificial intelligence can analyze large data sets to provide personalized recommendations based on previous shopping or browsing behavior, thereby improving the overall shopping experience.

Self-service options: AI allows customers to help themselves through different channels such as online chat, social networks or messaging apps, providing a direct and accessible self- service experience. Managing customer expectations in the age of artificial intelligence requires recognizing immediate needs and responding effectively. Artificial intelligence technologies such as conversational artificial intelligence can significantly improve communication, reduce response time, personalize experiences, and provide self-service options, thereby improving customer satisfaction and loyalty status.

As artificial intelligence continues to develop, its role in shaping customer experiences in social media marketing will become increasingly important.

CHAPTER 2

ARTIFICIAL INTELLIGENCE IN SOCIAL MEDIA

Integrating artificial intelligence (AI) into social media is a transformative step for brands, offering benefits from content creation to targeted advertising and greater customer involvement. Artificial intelligence in the social media market is expected to witness significant growth, demonstrating its growing importance in marketing strategies. When we talk about social AI we are referring to the use of artificial intelligence to mimic human intelligence, enabling machines to perform tasks such as problem solving, language understanding, and object speech recognition. This technology is already part of everyday tools, from smartphones to online recommendation systems. Machine learning, a subset of artificial intelligence, allows machines to make predictions based on large data sets and improve their accuracy over time. This aspect of artificial intelligence-the ability to learn and adapt without direct human intervention-is what makes it so powerful in social media marketing.

Accelerates revenue: AI can analyze data on social media audiences to improve engagement, discover new trends, and target potential buyers more effectively.

Cost reduction: Artificial intelligence automates content creation and management, making social media marketing more effective and profitable and much less costly.

AI APPLICATIONS IN SOCIAL MEDIA

Content creation and management: AI tools can automatically create and schedule social media content, including hashtags and links, thus simplifying the content distribution process.

Listening: artificial intelligence-based tools can analyze social data to track brand mentions, consumer trends and audience engagement, providing valuable information for strategy optimization.

Social Ad optimization: AI can write and optimize social ads, predicting which ones will perform best.

Influencer Marketing: AI helps identify the right influencers by analyzing social media analytics and can even create AI influencers for transparent brand representation.

The challenges of integrating artificial intelligence

Although artificial intelligence offers many advantages, its integration into existing social media strategies requires careful planning and technological expertise. Brands need to consider technical aspects, data quality, and the balance between automation and human contact. Understanding the process of integrating artificial intelligence into social media is essential for marketers who wish to leverage this technology effectively. By leveraging the capabilities of artificial intelligence, brands can improve their social media presence, interact with their audiences more effectively and achieve better marketing results. As artificial intelligence continues to develop, its role in shaping social media strategies will become increasingly important, offering new opportunities for innovation and engagement.

Choose the right artificial intelligence tools and technologies for social media integration

In the evolving social media landscape, choosing the right artificial intelligence (AI) tools and technologies is essential for effective integration. With the countless AI tools available, it is essential to choose those that fit your social media goals and strategy.

Key considerations for AI tool selection.

Consistency and quality: Consistency in posting quality content is essential for success on social media. Artificial intelligence tools can support your strategy by creating content, analyzing sentiment and providing Big Data insights, helping you make better decisions and understand your audience.

Content creation with artificial intelligence: Some artificial intelligence tools offer content recycling and conditional publishing, allowing existing content to be reused in creative ways. This helps maintain a steady stream of relevant content on your social networks.

Integration with multiple channels: Tools such as Vista Social allow integration with multiple social media platforms, providing a centralized system for managing your social media presence. This is especially useful for those who operate on multiple channels.

Effective campaign management: Tools such as Buffer simplify the planning of publishing campaigns on different channels, helping you maintain a balance between recurring and new content.

Social listening and audience insights: artificial intelligence tools such as Audiense focus on intelligent social listening, particularly on platforms such as Twitter, providing in-depth analysis of audience data.

Content creation and hashtag writing: tools such as Ocoya and Predis.ai help you write captions, create carousels and create videos, simplifying the content creation process.

Predictive analytics and performance optimization: the AI engine can predict the performance of future posts, helping you optimize your social media strategy to improve engagement and reach.

Evaluation of artificial intelligence tools for social media

Artificial intelligence capabilities: Look for tools with capabilities such as natural language processing, synthetic artificial intelligence, and predictive machine learning.

Ease of use and support: Choose easy-to-use tools and provide comprehensive support and documentation.

Integration features: Ensures that the tool integrates seamlessly with your favorite social media platforms.

Automation features: the tools provide time-saving features such as automated content planning and creation, which can significantly improve productivity.

Analysis and reporting: Choose tools that provide detailed engagement statistics and performance analysis.

Examples of effective artificial intelligence tools for social media

FeedHive: This tool excels in content recycling and conditional publishing. It uses an AI writing assistant to automatically create social media posts, complete with emoji and hashtags. FeedHive is especially useful for repurposing existing content and scheduling posts on different channels.

Social View: Ideal for managing multiple social media channels, Social View provides a comprehensive platform for scheduling posts, audience engagement, and monitoring reviews. Its artificial intelligence features help personalize content for different social media platforms, improving the relevance and impact of posts.

Buffer: Known for its user-friendly interface, Buffer allows you to plan and manage editorial campaigns across multiple channels. It allows you to create content arcs and maintain a balance between recurring and new content, ensuring a consistent and engaging social media presence.

Audiense: Focused on Twitter, Audiense offers social listening and in-depth audience analysis using artificial intelligence. It provides detailed reports on demographics, interests and engagement, allowing you to tailor your Twitter strategy for maximum impact.

Ocoya: This tool stands out for its artificial intelligence-based writing capabilities. Ocoya helps you create engaging captions and hashtags, saving you time and improving your social media content creation.

Predis.ai: Predis.ai is useful for creating visually appealing carousels and videos. It uses artificial intelligence to create content based on minimal input, making it ideal for creating visual content quickly and efficiently.

HootSuite: With multiple artificial intelligence-based features, HootSuite offers different publishing templates and helps you optimize your social media strategy. It is particularly effective for managing and analyzing social media campaigns on various platforms.

Choosing the right artificial intelligence tools for social media integration involves understanding your specific needs and evaluating the tools based on their functionality, ease of use, and integration capabilities. By choosing the right AI technology, you can improve your social media strategy, increase engagement and achieve better ROI. As artificial intelligence advances, its role in optimizing social media marketing strategies will become increasingly important, offering new opportunities for growth and engagement.

DATA COLLECTION AND ANALYSIS

In social media, the integration of artificial intelligence (AI) has revolutionized the way we collect and analyze data. This transformation is essential for understanding audience behavior, improving content personalization, and optimizing marketing strategies. The role of artificial intelligence in data collection and analysis Artificial intelligence in social media serves many purposes, from advertising management to content moderation. Here is how artificial intelligence is used to collect and analyze data: Ad management: AI tools analyze and target ad changes, perform customer segmentation to optimize ad translation strategies. This ensures that ads reach the most relevant audiences, increasing engagement and ROI.

Data analysis and labeling: artificial intelligence-based tools are capable of collecting, analyzing and labeling large amounts of user-generated data. This is important for both advertising and content moderation purposes as it helps to understand audience preferences and behavior.

Automated publishing and scheduling: the AI engine can schedule and publish content at optimal times, maximizing engagement. They analyze when their audience is most active and plan their posts accordingly.

Content generation: generative artificial intelligence is used to create social media posts, including text and images. It can also generate relevant hashtags for posts, which helps with visibility and content distribution.

Influencer Marketing: artificial intelligence tools of help identify the most suitable influencers for specific advertising campaigns by analyzing their demographics and audience reach.

Content moderation: artificial intelligence-based bots are used to filter out spam, content that violates guidelines, and inappropriate material.

This helps maintain the quality and integrity of content on the social platform.

Examples of artificial intelligence in social media platforms

Snapchat: Uses video filters and a general AI chatbot, My AI, to interact with users and recommend content.

Twitter: Uses artificial intelligence to recommend and moderate content, using tools such as IBM Watson for natural language processing.

Instagram: uses artificial intelligence for spam filtering, in-depth text analysis, and targeted advertising.

LinkedIn: Applying artificial intelligence to writing job descriptions and recommending content.

The benefits of artificial intelligence in social media include creating safer online environments, gathering customer sentiment, and personalizing content. However, risks such as AI-related bias, encouragement of echo chambers, and privacy concerns are also prevalent. Artificial intelligence algorithms used to moderate content can sometimes result in the accidental deletion or disappearance of inappropriate content. The impact of artificial intelligence on social media data collection and analysis is profound. Provides tools to better understand and engage audiences, optimize advertising strategies, and maintain content quality. However, addressing privacy concerns and misconceptions about artificial intelligence is essential to harness artificial intelligence responsibly in social media. As artificial intelligence technology continues to develop, its role in shaping social media strategies will become increasingly important, offering new opportunities for growth and engagement.

IMPLEMENTATION OF ARTIFICIAL INTELLIGENCE FOR CONTENT OPTIMIZATION

In the digital age, artificial intelligence has become "a tool that multiplies the power of creative expression", especially in creating content for social networks. The integration of artificial intelligence tools into social networks not only increases creativity, but also simplifies the content production process, making it more efficient and productive.

AI tools for social media content creation

Buffer AI assistant: This tool is an asset for creating endless variations of social media posts. It is especially useful for creating and reusing content across different platforms.AI assistants can translate posts into multiple languages and schedule them at optimal times, ensuring a consistent brand voice and maximizing engagement.

Narrated AI Content Genie: acts as a personal content marketer, this tool automatically creates content for social networks and blogs every week. Act as a strategist, creator and manager, especially useful for those who create content on their own. With more than 15 AI writing templates, it adapts to a variety of social media formats, including LinkedIn posts, Facebook and Instagram posts, and Twitter chats.

AI Caption Generator for Social Media HubSpot: This tool simplifies the process of creating engaging captions for social media. Create custom captions that match your brand personality and audience preferences, saving time valuable and improving engagement.

AI for listening and social engagement

Artificial intelligence tools also play an important role in social listening and audience engagement. They analyze conversations, mentions and trends, providing insights for a more targeted content strategy.

Buffer Engagement: this tool tracks audience engagement and uses machine learning to signal audience sentiment. It helps manage conversations and prioritize comments based on their relevance to your business.

Mentionlytics: artificial intelligence-based social listening tool to analyze online conversations and provide insights into audience sentiment, engagement, reach and more. Monitor brand mentions on social media and the Web, providing a comprehensive view of your brand's online presence.

AI for competitive analysis

Understanding your competitors' strategies is essential to optimizing your content. AI-based competitor analysis tools provide insights into content performance and audience engagement.

Predis.ai: Provides detailed competitive analysis for Facebook and Instagram, helping you understand the effectiveness of your competitors' content on social networks.

Rival IQ: This tool provides an in-depth analysis of your competitors, enabling you to make informed decisions about your social media content strategy. It provides comprehensive benchmarking data and tracks the performance of competitors' social media posts.

Images generated by artificial intelligence

Quality images are essential for creating engaging content on social media. Artificial intelligence algorithms can create stunning images based on the style of your brand.

Canva: Known for its intuitive interface, Canva now includes artificial intelligence features for graphic design, making it easier to create professional graphics for social media.

Enhance: Use artificial intelligence to enlarge and improve the resolution of images while maintaining the quality and attractiveness of the image content. Implementing artificial intelligence to optimize social media content means leveraging the right tools to improve creativity, efficiency, and effectiveness.

From creating visually appealing text to analyzing audience sentiment, artificial intelligence tools are changing the way we approach content creation on social media. As artificial intelligence technology continues to develop, its role in optimizing social media strategies will become increasingly important, presenting new opportunities for growth and engagement.

MONITORS AND ADJUSTS STRATEGY

In the rapidly evolving world of social media, artificial intelligence tools have become indispensable for marketers to optimize strategies, increase productivity and achieve positive ROI. It is essential to monitor and adapt these artificial intelligence strategies to ensure that they remain effective and relevant to evolving trends and audience preferences. The importance of artificial intelligence in social media strategy. Artificial intelligence in social media covers many different aspects, from content creation to analytics and advertising management. These tools help you gain a deeper understanding of your audience, improve efficiency in content creation, and optimize your social media campaigns.

The best artificial intelligence tools for social media strategy

Lately: This tool specializes in creating social media posts from broader content. It analyzes historical data to recommend the best release time for maximum impact. Lately is particularly useful for creating and scheduling content, ensuring consistent engagement.

Sprout Social: Ideal for community management, Sprout Social's automated technology helps you respond to your fans, customers or followers. It analyzes message wording and sentiment, suggesting automated responses that can be modified as needed.

HubSpot: HubSpot's social media software simplifies content creation and publishing using artificial intelligence. It automatically creates engaging social posts by analyzing metadata from the links provided, making it easy to maintain a consistent social presence.

Copy.ai: This tool automates the process of writing text for various social media platforms. This creates more publishing options, saves time and improves the quality of social media content.

Flick: Flick is designed to speed up content creation on social networks. It allows you to create custom captions and provides a content planning tool for Organizing ideas, simplifying the content creation process.

Emplifi: Formerly Socialbakers, Emplifi provides advanced audience insights and unified content feeds. It is particularly useful for influencer management as it offers an artificial intelligence-based influencer dashboard to simplify influencer collaboration processes.

Buffer AI Assistant: Buffer's engine can generate ideas for posts and content suitable for different social media platforms. Customize content by platform and audience, making it easy to create engaging posts.

The role of artificial intelligence in strategy optimization

Social media artificial intelligence tools are used not only to automate tasks but also to improve the overall strategy. These provide insights into your audience's behavior, suggest content improvements, and help you plan posts for optimal engagement. Regularly monitoring and adapting these artificial intelligence strategies is essential to ensure that they are in line with the latest audience trends and preferences. Integrating artificial intelligence into your social media strategy is a dynamic process that requires continuous monitoring and adjustment. Using artificial intelligence tools such as Lately, Sprout Social and HubSpot, marketers can optimize their social media presence, target audiences more effectively and achieve better ROI. As AI technology advances, its role in shaping and refining social media strategy will become increasingly important, offering new opportunities for growth and engagement. How artificial intelligence can personalize the user experience. The digital age has ushered in a new wave of customer interactions, and artificial intelligence-based personalization is at the forefront of improving the user experience. This approach uses artificial intelligence (AI) and machine learning to create highly personalized customer experiences by analyzing large amounts of data such as browsing history, social media interactions, and demographic information.

THE ESSENCE OF PERSONALIZATION BASED ON ARTIFICIAL INTELLIGENCE

Personalization based on artificial intelligence is about understanding the unique needs and preferences of each customer. An example of this approach is Amazon's recommendation system, which uses machine learning algorithms to analyze customer behavior and suggest products in real time. This will significantly increase engagement and sales.

Implementation of personalization based on artificial intelligence

In order to implement artificial intelligence-based personalization effectively, it is necessary to act in the following ways:

1. Set goals: Increase sales, improve customer satisfaction, reduce

churn rates, and more Have a clear understanding of why optimization is needed.

2. Use quality data: The success of artificial intelligence personalization depends largely on the quality and quantity of customer data.

3. Test and refine: Continuously test and refine your strategy based on customer feedback to remain relevant and effective.

4. Be transparent: Be transparent in your data collection and use it to build trust with your customers.

Personalization across all channels: Ensure that personalization is built into all customer touch points, including email, social media and in-store experiences.

Benefits of personalization based on artificial intelligence

Improving the customer experience: Personalizing the experience according to individual preferences increases customer satisfaction and loyalty.

Increased sales: Related product recommendations increase the likelihood of purchase.

Reduce customer churn: Personalized experiences foster customer loyalty. Data-driven insights: companies gain valuable insights into customer behavior to optimize their marketing strategies.

Case study on artificial intelligence-based personalization

Netflix: uses machine learning to recommend TV shows and movies based on viewing history, contributing to high engagement and retention.

Sephora: uses artificial intelligence to analyze customers' facial features and recommend the best makeup products, increasing customer satisfaction and trust.

Amazon: Introduced artificial intelligence for product recommendations, which has contributed significantly to the company's sales.

FUTURE TRENDS

Emerging trends include the use of voice assistants, chatbots, augmented reality (AR) and virtual reality (VR) for more engaging and personalized experiences. To lead the way in AI- based personalization, companies must focus on building high- quality data infrastructure and fostering a culture of innovation. AI-based personalization of represents a significant advancement for digital business, offering personalized customer experiences that drive increased engagement, sales and loyalty. However, implementation requires careful planning, high-quality data, and a focus on transparency and customer trust. As AI technology advances, the potential and effectiveness of personalized experiences will also increase.

Personalized content and recommendations through AI in social media

In today's digital landscape, content creators and marketers are increasingly turning to artificial intelligence to produce more personalized and engaging content for consumers. This shift is critical in an environment where users are bombarded with digital noise and are more selective in their reading and spending habits.

The role of artificial intelligence in improving content personalization

Artificial intelligence-based social media personalization uses technology to create, optimize and deliver content in tune with individual users. This approach is based on the analysis of large amounts of customer data, including browsing habits, purchases and Social media interactions.

The main ways in which artificial intelligence leverages personalization and content engagement

Industry-related predictive reporting: artificial intelligence tools such as obviously ai and Pecan provide insights into pricing plans, sales forecasts, and customer churn to help tailor your marketing strategies.

Analyzing competitors' tactics: tools such as Crayon and Klue enable companies to monitor competitors' online activities to inform strategic adjustments and product development.

Outreach content creation and distribution: AI customizes outreach messages, automates delivery, and optimizes campaign performance.

Customer segmentation: AI segments customers based on common characteristics beyond demographics, enabling more targeted and personalized marketing strategies.

Search engine optimization (SEO): Artificial intelligence identifies high-quality keywords and relevant websites for link building and improves content visibility.

Automatic distribution on the right platforms: Artificial intelligence-based content developers determine the best time to publish content on various social media platforms.

Personalized campaigns: artificial intelligence-based segmentation of enables targeted ads and personalized emails, increasing the chances of conversion.

Well-designed chatbots: conversational artificial intelligence in chatbots creates a more engaging user experience and provides personalized interactions and support.

EXAMPLES OF AI IN ACTION

Levi Strauss & Co: Developed the BOOST engine for inventory management and order fulfillment, using artificial intelligence to predict demand and personalize marketing.

JP Morgan Chase Bank: Collaboration with Persado to use artificial intelligence to improve communication with customers, resulting in increased engagement.

Although artificial intelligence brings many benefits to content personalization, challenges such as data protection, implementation costs and integration into existing systems must be considered. Companies need to ensure compliance with data protection regulations and seamlessly integrate artificial intelligence into their marketing strategies. Artificial intelligence is revolutionizing the way companies approach content personalization on social media. Using artificial intelligence tools for forecasting, competitive analysis, customer segmentation and SEO, companies can create more personalized and engaging content. This approach not only improves the user experience, but also improves business results. As AI technology advances, its role in content personalization and customer engagement will become increasingly important, creating new opportunities for growth and innovation in social media marketing.

Artificial intelligence in user interaction and engagement in social media

Artificial intelligence (AI) has become an important part of the social media revolution, significantly increasing user interaction and engagement. As social media platforms such as Facebook, Twitter, Instagram, and TikTok continue to grow, the role of artificial intelligence in shaping these interactions will become increasingly important.

Custom content recommendations

Algorithms based on artificial intelligence are better able to understand user preferences, which is critical to the success of social media. By analyzing user behavior, likes, shares, clicks and demographic data, social media platforms can tailor content to individual interests and increase engagement. For example, Facebook's advertising revenue comes mainly from personalized ads, demonstrating the effectiveness of artificial intelligence in understanding user preferences.

Artificial intelligence-driven content curation algorithms

YouTube's artificial intelligence-based recommendation system is an excellent example of how machine learning and deep learning techniques can be used to curate content relevant to users' interests. This artificial intelligence approach has proven effective in retaining users, as a significant portion of time spent on YouTube comes from these recommendations. Personalized content recommendations lengthen user sessions and increase advertising revenue. Companies also benefit from more effective and targeted advertising, increasing conversion rates and sales. Personalized content fosters a sense of community and connection, as users are more likely to interact with content tailored to their preferences.

SENTIMENT ANALYSIS AND TREND FORECASTING

AI-based sentiment analysis tools measure audience sentiment by analyzing textual and visual content on social media. These tools help monitor brand perception and public opinion. Artificial intelligence algorithms also predict trends and identify content that has the potential to go viral, helping content creators and companies stay ahead of the curve. Sentiment analysis and social media trend forecasting provide valuable insights into your marketing strategy. With this information, companies can create more relevant and targeted content, increase customer engagement, and make informed decisions about product development and branding. AI has an important role to play in reinventing social media, recommending personalized content, improving customer service, and providing valuable insights into user behavior and market trends. As artificial intelligence technology advances, it will be important to balance personalization with privacy and address concerns about bias and manipulation. The integration of artificial intelligence into social media will continue to shape the digital landscape, influencing societies around the world and meeting the evolving needs and expectations of users.

Personalized advertising with artificial intelligence in social media

In the competitive online world, it is important to stand out from the crowd and connect with your target audience, and this is where artificial intelligence (AI) plays a key role. Using artificial intelligence, you can create personalized, targeted ads that resonate with your audience, improving results and conversions. To effectively leverage artificial intelligence in advertising, it is important to align artificial intelligence tools with your goals and simplify the process. A comprehensive AI marketing strategy requires defining goals, audience, message, and budget. Artificial intelligence can help in several ways:

Improve ad performance: Post relevant ads that resonate with your customers.

Generate more sales: Interact with existing customers more often and effectively.

Increases acquisition rates: targets new audiences based on preference and location.

But how do personalized ads work? Personalized ads use customer data, such as browsing behavior and purchase history, to create ads that respond directly to your audience's interests. AI targeting automates this process, enabling targeted targeting of specific customer segments and continuous optimization of campaigns.

STRATEGIES FOR TARGETED ADVERTISING

Customer segmentation: AI segments your customer base into groups for targeted advertising. Tools such as HubSpot's ChatSpot can help in this process.

Optimizing the buyer and customer journey: AI ads can naturally guide buyers through the purchase channel from awareness to decision-making.

Retargeting: AI Retargeting analyzes user behavior and delivers personalized ads. For example, Carrefour Taiwan used AI retargeting to improve the conversion rate of its website.

Email Marketing: AI analyzes your email campaign data and provides paid advertising text and images.

Social Listening: AI tracks mentions of your company and industry and provides insights for long-term planning.

Predictive analytics: Predict customer behavior and create ads based on artificial intelligence.

Artificial intelligence-based website personalization: Dynamically customize your website to increase engagement and conversions.

Use Google's artificial intelligence for paid ads: Use Google's dynamic ads and AI features for personalized ads.

Create personalized ads with Meta's artificial intelligence: Meta provides tools such as Automatic Ads and Audience Network to create personalized ads.

Personalization in AI-focused advertising is the key to campaign success. Artificial intelligence allows you to create ads that grab your audience's attention and produce great results. Implementing these strategies will optimize your campaigns, increase conversions and improve return on ad spend. As AI technology advances, its role in advertising will become increasingly important, creating new opportunities for growth and innovation in digital marketing. The integration of artificial intelligence (AI) into social media has led to the emergence of data feedback loops, a process by which customer data is continuously used to improve products and services. This cycle of collecting data, feeding it into machine learning algorithms, and using that information to acquire more customers is critical to improving user experience and engagement. Data feedback loops occur when companies collect customer data and use it to improve artificial intelligence algorithms. This process leads to better products and services, attracts more customers, and generates more data. For example, Google's search engine becomes more accurate and relevant as more people use it, creating a cycle of continuous improvement. The strength of these data feedback loops can vary widely. Companies can consciously choose to improve:

Product redesign: Create products or services that naturally generate user data that can be used to improve quality. For example, a smart thermostat learns from your preferences and adjusts temperature settings.

Integration with other products: combine products with other services to create richer data feedback loops. For example, wearable devices can be integrated into fitness apps to correlate exercise data with health parameters.

Solicit feedback from users: Gather feedback in a minimally invasive way and make the benefits clear to users. This helps us refine our artificial intelligence algorithms and improve the user experience.

Examples of effective data feedback loops

Google Maps: Uses route choices and travel times to improve route recommendations and traffic forecasts.

Spotify: Learn from users' playlist selections to improve music recommendation algorithms.

Fitbit: The data feedback loop is limited but could be improved by adding standardized fitness tests or integrating with other fitness products.

Challenges in creating data feedback loops

Creating effective data feedback loops can be difficult, especially for products where user feedback is difficult to track or where clear preferences are not revealed. Traditional products such as cars and clothing that are not digitally connected rely on manual methods of collecting feedback such as surveys, which limit the speed and scope of improvement. Data feedback loops are a key part of artificial intelligence in social media, enabling continuous improvement and personalization of the user experience. By understanding and strengthening these connections, a sustainable competitive advantage can be created. As AI technology advances, the ability to effectively leverage data feedback loops to deliver personalized and engaging user experiences on social media platforms will become increasingly important.

CHAPTER 3

ARTIFICIAL INTELLIGENCE TOOLS FOR SOCIAL MEDIA MARKETING

Advent of artificial intelligence (AI) in advertising, particularly on social media, is revolutionizing the way brands interact with their audiences. The role of artificial intelligence in advertising ranges from analyzing data to creating personalized advertising experiences. Artificial intelligence in social media advertising is the use of technology to make advertising more targeted, efficient and effective. We use machine learning algorithms to analyze user data, predict behavior, and deliver personalized advertising content. The main aspects of artificial intelligence in social media advertising are:

Targeted advertising: artificial intelligence algorithms analyze user data such as interests, browsing history and interaction patterns to create highly targeted advertising campaigns. This allows your ads to be shown to users who are most likely to be interested in your product or service, increasing your chances of conversion.

Dynamic content creation: artificial intelligence tools can generate creative content for advertising, such as images and text, tailored to individual users. This dynamic content creation creates more engaging and relevant ads.

Predictive analytics: ai uses predictive analytics to predict future consumer behavior, enabling advertisers to anticipate market trends and user needs.

Automated bidding and optimization: artificial intelligence systems can automate the bidding process on ad platforms, optimizing ad spend and maximizing ROI. They continuously analyze campaign performance and make changes in real time.

Improved user experience: AI improves the overall user experience on social media platforms by personalizing ads. Users see ads more relevant to their interests, which can increase their positive perception of promoted brands.

Examples of artificial intelligence tools in social media advertising

Google Ads AI: provides tools for automated bidding and ad performance optimization.

Facebook Ads AI: Uses user data to create personalized advertising experiences on Facebook and Instagram.

Adobe Teacher: helps you create AI-based marketing content and insights.

Challenges and ethical considerations

Although artificial intelligence offers many advantages, there are also challenges, such as ensuring user privacy and avoiding algorithmic bias. Advertisers must address these challenges responsibly, be transparent and adhere to ethical standards. Artificial intelligence is changing the landscape of social media advertising, providing tools for targeted advertising, content creation and campaign optimization. As AI technology advances, its role in improving advertising strategies and user experience on social media platforms will become increasingly important, offering new opportunities for growth and innovation in digital marketing. When it comes to social media marketing, identifying the right target group is critical to the success of a campaign. Artificial intelligence (AI) has revolutionized this, making it more accurate and efficient. Artificial intelligence is changing the way marketers identify and understand their audiences. By analyzing large amounts of data, artificial intelligence algorithms can segment your audience based on various factors such as demographics, interests, online behavior and interaction patterns.

HOW ARTIFICIAL INTELLIGENCE IMPROVES TARGET AUDIENCE IDENTIFICATION

In-depth data analysis: AI examines social media data to Derive insights into user preferences, behaviors, a n d trends. This detailed analysis helps you create profiles of detailed audiences.

Modeling predictive: The artificial uses predictive analytics to predict the future behavior and preferences of the consumers. This allows marketers to anticipate needs and adjust campaigns accordingly.

Segmentation and personalization: Artificial intelligence segments target groups into different groups with similar characteristics. This segmentation enables more personalized and effective marketing strategies.

Real-time insights: Artificial intelligence provides real-time insights into audience behavior, enabling marketers to quickly make data-driven decisions.

Increased engagement: AI helps you create messages and content that resonate with users by better understanding your audience, resulting in higher engagement rates.

Artificial intelligence tools for audience identification

Google Analytics: Provides advanced audience information and segmentation features.

Facebook Insights: provides detailed demographic, geographic and psychographic data on your Facebook audience.

Hootsuite Insights: uses artificial intelligence to analyze social media conversations to identify audience sentiment and trends.

The impact of AI on target group identification. The impact of AI on target group identification is significant. This not only makes the process more efficient, but also more accurate. Marketers can now deliver the right message to the right people at the right time, greatly increasing the effectiveness of their campaigns. However, while artificial intelligence has many advantages, it also presents challenges, such as ensuring data privacy and avoiding bias in data analysis. Marketers must use artificial intelligence responsibly, adhering to ethical standards and regulations. Artificial intelligence to identify target groups will revolutionize social media marketing. As AI technology advances, its role in improving audience identification and segmentation will become increasingly important, offering new opportunities for targeted and effective marketing campaigns.

CREATION AND OPTIMIZATION OF ADS

Artificial intelligence (AI) is more than just a buzzword in social media marketing; it is a powerful tool that is reshaping the way ads are created and optimized. AI-based ad creation and optimization uses intelligent algorithms to create and personalize ad content to ensure it resonates effectively with your target audience.

The role of artificial intelligence in the creation and optimization of advertising

Automated content creation: Artificial intelligence tools can generate advertising content, including text and images, tailored to specific audience segments. Automation speeds up the creative process and ensures message consistency.

Dynamic ad personalization: Artificial intelligence algorithms analyze user data and personalize ads in real time. This means that ads change based on user interaction, making them more relevant and engaging.

Predictive performance analytics: AI predicts the performance of different ad variants, enabling marketers to optimize campaigns before they are launched.

Real-time optimization: Once your ads start running, artificial intelligence continuously analyzes performance data and makes changes to improve engagement and conversion rates.

Examples of artificial intelligence tools for creating and optimizing advertisements

Google responsive search ads: These ads automatically test different combinations of titles and descriptions and learn which combinations work best.

Dynamic Facebook Ads: Customize ads based on user behavior and preferences, optimizing ad serving for users most likely to take action.

Adobe Teacher: uses artificial intelligence to simplify the ad creation process and provides tools for image editing, personalization, and performance analysis.

The impact of artificial intelligence on ad creation and optimization. The impact of artificial intelligence in this area is significant.

It not only simplifies the creative process, but also ensures better advertising effectiveness.

Using artificial intelligence, marketers can create ads that are not only visually appealing but also targeted and personalized.

PERFORMANCE TRACKING WITH AI ANALYTICS

In the dynamic world of social media marketing, it is important to understand and measure the performance of campaigns. Artificial intelligence (AI) has significantly improved this problem through advanced analytics that provide in-depth information and more accurate performance monitoring. Artificial intelligence has transformed performance monitoring from a reactive to a proactive approach. Using artificial intelligence analytics, marketers can not only measure but also predict campaign performance, leading to more informed decisions.

Key features of artificial intelligence in performance monitoring

Real-time data analysis: Artificial intelligence tools analyze data in real time, providing immediate insight into campaign performance. This allows marketers to make quick changes to optimize results.

Predictive analytics: Artificial intelligence can predict future trends based on current data, helping marketers anticipate changes in consumer behavior and adjust strategies accordingly.

Advanced segmentation and insights: Artificial intelligence algorithms segment audience data more precisely, providing insights into different customer groups and their interactions with your content.

Automated reporting: Artificial intelligence tools automate the reporting process, generating comprehensive reports that highlight key performance indicators (KPIs) and metrics.

Artificial intelligence tools for performance monitoring

Google Analytics: Provides advanced artificial intelligence- based insights into website traffic, user behavior and campaign performance.

Sprout Social: provides detailed analysis of social media engagement, audience growth, and content performance.

Hootsuite Insights: uses artificial intelligence to track brand mentions, sentiment analysis and audience demographics across multiple social media platforms.

AI-based analytics provide a deeper understanding of campaign performance. Marketers can see what works and what doesn't in real time, enabling them to continuously optimize their strategies. AI has revolutionized performance monitoring in social media marketing. Artificial intelligence enables marketers to monitor and optimize campaigns more effectively than ever before by providing real-time data analysis, predictive insights, and automated reporting. As AI technology advances, its role in improving performance monitoring and analysis will become increasingly important, offering new opportunities for growth and success in the digital marketing landscape.

CONTENT CREATION WITH AI

Artificial intelligence (AI) is revolutionizing content creation in social media marketing, offering new ways to engage audiences with innovative and personalized content. To realize the full potential of artificial intelligence, it is important to understand how it contributes to content creation. Artificial intelligence in content creation involves the use of algorithms and machine learning to generate, optimize and personalize content. This technology can analyze trends, understand user preferences and create content that resonates with specific audiences.

How artificial intelligence improves content creation

Automatic content generation: AI tools can automatically generate text, images and videos. This automation ensures a consistent flow of content, saving time and resources.

Personalization at scale: AI analyzes user data and personalizes content for different audience segments. This creates more engaging and relevant content that resonates with your audience.

Content optimization: AI can optimize your content for different platforms, ensuring that it meets the specific needs and preferences of each social media channel.

Content performance prediction: artificial intelligence tools predict the performance of different types of content, allowing marketers to focus on the most effective strategies.

The impact of artificial intelligence on content creation

The impact of artificial intelligence on content creation is significant. This not only simplifies the creative process, but also makes your content more effective and engaging. Using artificial intelligence, marketers can create content that is not only visually appealing, but also targeted and personalized.

AI for generating written content in social media marketing

Artificial intelligence (AI) is changing the way written content is created for social media marketing. Artificial intelligence tools can now generate engaging, high- quality text, making content creation more efficient and effective.

The benefits of artificial intelligence in writing

The role of artificial intelligence in generating written content is multifaceted. From social media posts to blog articles, you can create different types of content tailored to specific audience segments and platforms.

Efficiency and speed: The artificial intelligence of greatly accelerates the content creation process, creating drafts in seconds. This allows marketers to focus on strategy and creativity.

Consistency and scalability: AI ensures a consistent tone and style throughout your content. You can also increase content production without compromising quality.

Personalization: AI tools analyze user data and create personalized content that resonates with different audiences.

SEO Optimization: Many AI writing tools can optimize your content for search engines and improve your online visibility.

Examples of AI writing tools

OpenAI's GPT-3: a tool that can produce advanced language models that can generate human-like text. It helps you create blog posts, social media updates and more.

Grammarly: is more than just a grammar checker. It uses artificial intelligence to improve the clarity, attractiveness and distribution of written content.

Copy.ai: Specializes in creating marketing copy, from product descriptions to advertising copy and social media posts.

Jarvis (Conversion.ai): Artificial intelligence tool created by marketing experts to help you generate engaging content converting.

The impact of artificial intelligence on content writing

The impact of artificial intelligence on content creation is significant. It provides a new level of efficiency, enabling marketers to create more content in less time. AI-generated content is highly engaging because it is tailored to the interests and preferences of the audience. Artificial intelligence for generating written content is a breakthrough in social media marketing. It simplifies the content creation process and ensures efficiency, consistency and personalization. As AI technology advances, its role in content creation will become increasingly important, offering new opportunities for innovation and engagement in digital marketing.

Artificial intelligence in creating visual content for social media marketing

The artificial intelligence (AI) is revolutionizing the creation of visual and written content in social media marketing. AI tools now can generate and enhance images and videos to make them more attractive and relevant to a specific audience. AI's involvement in visual content creation ranges from automating the design process to customizing of images based on users' preferences and behaviors.

Automatic image and video generation: Artificial intelligence can create high-quality images and videos, reducing the need for graphic design resources.

Personalization: Artificial intelligence analyzes user engagement and adapts images to audience preferences, making content more relevant and impactful.

Enhance and edit: AI tools can improve the quality of your images and videos, including color correction, resizing, and style adjustments.

Content optimization: AI optimizes visual content for various social media platforms to ensure that it meets specific format and size requirements.

Examples of artificial intelligence tools for creating visual content

Canva Visual Magic Tools: provides artificial intelligence-based design suggestions and simplifies the creation of professional social media graphics.

Adobe Spark: Uses artificial intelligence to automate the design process and help you create visually appealing social media posts, Web pages, and short videos.

Lumens5: Uses artificial intelligence to convert text content into an engaging video format, perfect for creating video content for social media platforms. The impact of artificial intelligence in this field is profound. It not only makes the creation process more efficient, but also makes the visual presentation more effective and engaging. Using artificial intelligence, marketers can create images that are not only aesthetically pleasing, but also targeted and personalized.

Content optimization for SEO and engagement with artificial intelligence in social media marketing

In the world of digital marketing, it is important to create content that ranks high in search engines and attracts an audience on social media. Artificial intelligence (AI) plays a key role in content optimization for both SEO (search engine optimization) and user engagement.

The intersection of AI, SEO, and engagement: Artificial intelligence improves content optimization by analyzing large amounts of data to understand what resonates with your audience and what ranks higher in search engines. These two goals make your content not only detectable, but also engaging.

How artificial intelligence improves content optimization

Keyword analysis and integration: AI tools identify trending keywords and suggest optimal placement within your content to improve SEO without sacrificing readability.

Relevance and quality of content: AI assesses the quality and relevance of content to ensure that it matches the user's search intent and preferences. This is important for both SEO and engagement.

User engagement analysis: Artificial intelligence of analyzes how users interact with your content, providing insights into what works and what doesn't and enabling continuous improvement.

Predictive analysis of *trending topics*: Artificial intelligence predicts future trends and helps marketers create content that attracts users and ranks well.

AI tools for content optimization

SEMrush: Provides comprehensive SEO tools based on artificial intelligence, including keyword research, Web site checks, content suggestions and more.

MarketMuse: Use artificial intelligence to analyze your content and provide recommendations for improvement in terms of SEO and user engagement.

Surfer SEO: an artificial intelligence-based tool that analyzes content, compares it with top-level pages, and provides guidelines for optimization.

The impact of artificial intelligence on content optimization

The impact of artificial intelligence in this field is significant. This not only simplifies the optimization process, but also ensures that your content reaches your target audience and engages them more effectively. Artificial intelligence enables marketers to create SEO-friendly and engaging content.

CHATBOT AND CUSTOMER SERVICE WITH AI

In the social media marketing space, AI-powered chatbots have emerged as an important tool to revolutionize customer service and engagement. These AI-based chatbots are more than just automated responses; they are sophisticated systems that can understand and interact with users in a more human way. Artificial intelligence-based chatbots on social media serve a variety of purposes, from answering customer questions to providing personalized advice to managing transactions. 24/7 Customer Interaction: AI chatbots are available 24 hours a day and respond immediately to the customer questions. This is important to maintain customer satisfaction and loyalty. These chatbots can analyze user data and past interactions to provide personalized responses and suggestions to improve the user experience. They can also handle many applications at once, making them especially advantageous for companies with a large customer base. In addition, the latter also serve to capture valuable customer data that can be used to improve marketing strategies and better understand customer preferences.

Examples of AI Chatbot tools

Chatfuel: specializes in creating AI chatbots for Facebook Messenger that enable companies to automate responses and interact effectively with customers.

ManyChat: ManyChat is another popular tool for creating chatbots on Facebook Messenger, offering an easy-to-use interface and a variety of customer engagement features.

Drift: provides AI chatbots for website customer service, helping companies interact with website visitors in real time.

The impact of AI chatbots on social media marketing is significant. Not only will your customer service be more efficient, but they will also increase your customers' retention and loyalty. By using AI chatbots, companies can ensure a consistent and personalized customer experience. Although AI-powered chatbots have many advantages, they also present challenges, such as maintaining a balance between automated responses and human touch. It is also important to ensure the privacy and security of customer data collected by chatbots. AI chatbots represent an important advance in social media marketing, offering ways to improve customer service efficiency, personalize user experiences and collect valuable data. As AI technology continues to evolve, chatbots will become even more capable and effective in social media marketing, offering companies new ways to interact with customers. Introducing AI chatbots into customer interactions in social media marketing is a strategic move that will significantly improve customer engagement and support. These artificial intelligence-based chatbots are designed to interact with customers in a conversational manner, providing immediate responses and personalized support.

Steps to implement AI chatbots

1. Define your goals: Be clear about what you want your chatbot to accomplish, such as handling customer inquiries, providing product recommendations or facilitating transactions.

2. Choose the right platform: Choose a chatbot platform that fits your social media strategy and audience preferences. Think about where your customers are most active. Facebook, Twitter, Instagram or website.

3. Design the conversation flow: Map the conversations your chatbot might have with your users. This includes greeting people, answering frequently asked questions, and answering complex questions that require human intervention.

4. Personalize your chatbot experience: Use artificial intelligence to

personalize interactions based on user data and previous interactions. This might include addressing you by name or providing recommendations based on your browsing history.

5. Integration with existing systems: Ensure that chatbots are integrated with CRM and other related systems to ensure seamless data exchange and improved service.

6. Chatbot testing and training : Before you put your chatbot into production , test it thoroughly to make sure it responds accurately and effectively.

7. Continuously train your chatbot with new data to improve performance.

Examples of AI chatbot tools

MobileMonkey: Provides a variety of chatbot services for various platforms, including Facebook Messenger, with features such as lead generation and customer support.

Botsify: is an easy-to-use chatbot generator that enables integration with a variety of platforms and provides artificial intelligence-based conversation capabilities.

Zendesk Chat: Known for its customer service features, Zendesk Chat offers an AI chatbot that can be integrated into social media platforms and Web sites.

AI chatbots can significantly improve customer interactions on social media. Provide immediate support to your customers, reduce response time, and handle many requests at once. This improves customer satisfaction and leaves human customer service agents more time to handle more complex problems. AI chatbots are valuable tools for improving customer interactions in social media marketing. By carefully implementing and continuously improving these chatbots, companies can provide better customer service, personalize the user experience and increase overall customer engagement on social media platforms. As AI technology advances, the potential for chatbots to transform customer service continues to grow. Artificial intelligence for personalized customer service in social media marketing Artificial intelligence (AI) is redefining customer service in social media marketing by providing personalized, efficient and responsive service. AI-based tools can understand and meet the needs of individual customers, improving the overall customer experience.

The role of artificial intelligence in personalizing customer service

Artificial intelligence in customer service goes beyond automated responses. Understanding your customers' preferences, history, and behavior is critical to providing personalized care.

Understanding customer preferences: Artificial intelligence analyzes past interactions and preferences to provide the right support to each customer. This may include product recommendations or answers to specific questions based on your previous purchases.

24/7 availability: the AI chatbot is available 24 hours a day to provide immediate support to your customers at any time. This is extremely important in today's fast-paced digital environment.

Consistent and accurate answers: Artificial intelligence ensures consistency in the information provided, reduces the possibility of error human and improves the reliability of customer service.

Seamless integration with social media platforms: This AI tools are designed to integrate seamlessly with various social media platforms, ensuring a seamless customer service experience across all channels.

Artificial intelligence tools for personalized customer service

Intercom: offers artificial intelligence-based chatbots that provide personalized customer support and integrate with social media platforms.

Answer Bot from Zendesk: uses machine learning to understand customer questions and provide accurate, personalized answers.

Drift: Conversational marketing and sales companies offer artificial intelligence-based chatbots that personalize interactions based on user behavior and data.

The impact of artificial intelligence on customer service.

The introduction of artificial intelligence in customer service is changing the way companies interact with their customers. Personalized and timely support leads to greater customer satisfaction. In addition, artificial intelligence enables human customer service agents to handle more complex problems, increasing overall efficiency.

Evaluate and improve the performance of chatbots in social media marketing

In the social media marketing environment, the effectiveness of artificial intelligence-based chatbots is critical to maintaining high-quality customer service. To ensure that your chatbot meets your customers' needs and improves the overall experience of the user, it is essential to regularly evaluate and improve the performance of your chatbot.

Key aspects of chatbot performance evaluation

User interaction analysis: Monitoring how users interact with your chatbot provides information about its effectiveness. This includes analysis of response rates, call times and user satisfaction.

Accuracy and relevance of response: Assessing the accuracy and relevance of a chatbot's responses helps determine whether the chatbot actually understands and responds to the user's questions.

Escalation rate: Monitoring how often users need to be transferred from the chatbot to a human agent will highlight areas where the chatbot needs improvement.

Gather user feedback: Direct user feedback helps you evaluate your chatbot's performance and identify opportunities for improvement.

Tools for evaluating chatbot performance

Chatbase: Provides chatbot-specific analysis to help identify common user questions and determine the effectiveness of chatbot responses.

Dashbot: provides detailed analytics for your chatbot, including conversation analysis, sentiment analysis, and user engagement metrics.

Botanlytics: focuses on conversation analysis, providing insights into user interactions and chatbot performance.

Strategies for improving chatbot performance

Regular training and updates: Continuous updating of the chatbot's knowledge base and training with new data ensure its effectiveness and up-to-dateness.

Improved personalization: Improving the chatbot's ability to offer personalized responses based on user data can significantly improve the user experience.

Integration of natural language processing (NLP): Advanced NLP enables chatbots to understand and answer users' questions more accurately and naturally.

Optimizing the user journey: Streamlining the flow of conversation to make interactions more intuitive and efficient can improve user satisfaction.

Finally, let us look together at the challenges that can arise when optimizing the performance of a chatbot. The latter presents challenges such as enabling chatbots to handle complex questions and maintaining a balance between automated responses and human-like interactions. It is also important to ensure user privacy and data security. Evaluating and improving chatbot performance is an ongoing process in social media marketing. With the right tools and strategies, companies can improve their chatbots and make them more efficient, accurate and easy to use. As AI technology advances, chatbots have the potential to transform customer service, offering companies new ways to interact effectively with their audiences.

CHAPTER 4

CREATION OF AN INTEGRATED MARKETING STRATEGY

Integrating artificial intelligence (AI) into your marketing strategy is a strategic move that can improve significantly the effectiveness of your marketing efforts. However, it requires careful planning and consideration to ensure alignment with overall business objectives. Intelligence artificial in marketing is not limited only to the introduction of new technologies. It involves using artificial intelligence to obtain detailed information about customer behavior, optimize marketing campaigns and improve the customer experience. This requires a strategic approach to ensure that artificial intelligence integration is in line with a company's marketing objectives.

Stages of strategic planning of AI integration

1. Define clear goals: use AI to identify the goals you wish to achieve. Examples include increasing customer loyalty, personalizing marketing messages, and increasing the efficiency of advertising campaigns.

2. Assess your current capabilities: Assess your current marketing

infrastructure and capabilities to understand where you can effectively integrate artificial intelligence.

3. Identify the right AI tools: Choose AI tools that align with your marketing goals. This includes artificial intelligence for data analysis, content creation, customer service or personalized advertising.

4. Data infrastructure: make sure you have the necessary data infrastructure to support AI. This includes data collection, storage and analysis capabilities.

5. Skills development and training: invest in training your team to use AI tools effectively.

6. Understanding the capabilities and limitations of artificial intelligence is important for successful integration.

7. Pilot project: Start with a small pilot project to test the effectiveness of artificial intelligence in your marketing strategy. This allows you to make changes and improvements before the full launch.

8. Continuous monitoring and adjustment: Regularly monitor the performance of your artificial intelligence tools and adjust your strategy as needed. Artificial intelligence is not a forgotten solution; it requires ongoing management and optimization.

Examples of artificial intelligence tools for marketing strategy

HubSpot: Provides artificial intelligence-based marketing automation tools for personalized e-mail marketing and customer relationship management.

Salesforce Einstein: Provide artificial intelligence-based insights into your customer data to create more targeted marketing campaigns.

Google Analytics: Uses artificial intelligence to provide advanced data analysis and insights into website traffic and user behavior.

To realize the full potential of AI technology, strategic planning for integrating AI into marketing is essential. By clearly defining goals, choosing the right tools and continuously monitoring performance, companies can effectively integrate artificial intelligence into their marketing strategies to increase efficiency, customer loyalty and overall marketing success. As AI technology advances, its role in the development of marketing strategies becomes increasingly important.

ARTIFICIAL INTELLIGENCE IN EMAIL MARKETING

Artificial intelligence (AI) is revolutionizing email marketing, turning it into a more dynamic, personalized and effective customer engagement tool. By integrating artificial intelligence into email marketing strategies, companies can significantly improve the relevance and impact of their communications. Artificial intelligence in email marketing involves the use of intelligent algorithms to personalize content, optimize send times and segment target groups more effectively. This increases open rates, increases engagement, and increases conversions.

How artificial intelligence improves e-mail marketing

Personalized content: Artificial intelligence analyzes customer data and creates highly personalized emails. This may include personalized product recommendations, personal greetings or content based on the recipient's previous interactions.

Optimal timing: AI determines the best time to send e- mails to each recipient, increasing the likelihood that your e- mails will be opened and read.

Audience segmentation: AI segments your email list based on customer behavior, preferences and engagement, enabling more targeted and relevant email campaigns.

Automated A/B testing: AI can automatically test different versions of your email content to determine which works best and continuously optimize your e- mail campaigns.

Predictive analytics: artificial intelligence predicts customer behavior and preferences, enabling marketers to anticipate needs and adapt email content accordingly.

Artificial intelligence tools for e-mail marketing

Mailchimp AI: offers features such as send time optimization and content personalization to make your email campaigns more effective.

ActiveCampaign: Use artificial intelligence for predictive delivery and content recommendations to improve the relevance of your email communications.

HubSpot E-mail Marketing: provides artificial intelligence- based insights for audience segmentation and optimization of your e-mail campaigns.

The impact of artificial intelligence on email marketing is significant. This not only makes your e-mail campaigns more efficient, but also allows you to better tailor them to the interests and needs of your audience. Using artificial intelligence, anyone can create email campaigns that are not only more attractive, but also more likely to generate conversions.

AI FOR SEO CUSTOMIZATION

Artificial intelligence (AI) is changing the landscape of search engine optimization (SEO), a key part of your digital marketing strategy. The ability of artificial intelligence to analyze large amounts of data and predict trends has proven invaluable in optimizing Web sites to improve search engine rankings. Artificial intelligence in SEO involves the use of algorithms and machine learning to understand search engine behavior, optimize content and improve website visibility. This approach leads to a more effective and efficient SEO strategy.

The main ways in which artificial intelligence improves SEO

Keyword analysis and optimization: AI tools identify trending keywords and suggest the most effective ways to integrate them into your website content to improve ranking in search results.

Relevance and quality of content: Artificial Intelligence evaluates content and suggests improvements to ensure it is in line with search intent and user preferences, a key element of SEO.

User Experience Optimization: Artificial Intelligence analyzes user behavior on your website and suggests changes that can improve the user experience. This is a factor that search engines consider when ranking websites.

Backlink analysis: artificial intelligence tools can analyze backlink profiles to identify potential opportunities for high-quality links and link building strategies.

Predictive analytics: artificial intelligence predicts future SEO trends and helps marketers stay one step ahead in optimizing their websites.

AI tools for SEO optimization

SEMrush: offers artificial intelligence-based SEO tools such as keyword research, Web site audits, and competitive analysis.

Moz Pro: uses artificial intelligence to provide insights into keyword placement, link building opportunities, and site crawling.

Ahrefs: Enhances artificial intelligence for comprehensive backlink analysis, keyword research and content exploration.

The impact of artificial intelligence on SEO

The impact of artificial intelligence on SEO will be transformative. This not only simplifies the SEO process, but also makes your strategy more data-driven and more aligned with search engine algorithms. Using artificial intelligence, one can improve search engine rankings, increase organic traffic and improve online visibility. Artificial intelligence for SEO optimization is a breakthrough in digital marketing. This allows you to develop a more effective data-driven SEO strategy, leading to better search rankings and online visibility. As AI technology advances, its role in SEO will become increasingly important, offering new opportunities for growth and success in digital marketing. Integrating artificial intelligence (AI) into your marketing strategy means not only using cutting-edge technologies, but also aligning AI capabilities with your overall business goals. This collaboration ensures that artificial intelligence not only supports but also improves a company's strategic goals. The key to successfully integrating artificial intelligence into your marketing strategy is to understand how it can help you achieve specific business goals, such as increasing sales, boosting customer loyalty and increasing brand awareness.

Steps to align AI with goals

Identification of goals: Clearly define the goals you want to achieve. These include goals such as expanding the market, building customer loyalty, and increasing sales.

Evaluation of AI capabilities: understand AI capabilities with respect to your goals. This involves assessing how artificial intelligence can improve customer information, optimize marketing campaigns, and improve customer service.

Select relevant AI tools: Select AI tools in line with your goals. For example, if your goal is to increase customer loyalty, a tool that analyzes customer behavior and personalizes content is ideal.

Integrate AI into your existing processes: seamlessly integrate AI tools into your existing marketing processes. In this way, artificial intelligence does not work alone, but complements and enhances existing strategies.

Train your team: help your team understand how to use AI tools effectively and how they can help you achieve your business goals.

Measure and adapt: regularly measure the impact of artificial intelligence on your marketing activities and adapt your strategy as needed to ensure alignment with your business goals.

In addition, to maximize the potential of AI technology, it remains important for marketing to align AI with business objectives. By carefully selecting and integrating artificial intelligence tools into your marketing strategy, you can ensure that artificial intelligence not only supports, but promotes your business goals. As artificial intelligence continues to evolve, its role in aligning and achieving business goals will become increasingly important, offering new opportunities for strategic growth and success. Integrating artificial intelligence (AI) into marketing strategies is a pioneering step, but it also presents its own challenges. Understanding and overcoming these challenges is critical to successfully implementing artificial intelligence into your marketing strategy.

Key challenges in implementing the AI strategy

Privacy and security: artificial intelligence systems rely heavily on data; therefore, it is important to ensure the privacy and security of client information.

Complying with data protection laws and maintaining customer trust are the main challenges Integration into existing systems: Integrating artificial intelligence tools into existing marketing systems and processes can be complex. It is important to ensure compatibility and minimize disruption to ongoing operations.

Skills and training gap: Effective use of AI requires specific skills and knowledge. Overcoming skills gaps within your team and providing adequate training can be difficult.

Allocation of costs and resources: Implementation of solutions of artificial intelligence often involves significant investments in costs and resources. Balancing these investments with expected returns is a key challenge.

Managing expectations: There can be a gap between expectations of AI and actual capabilities. It is important to consider stakeholders' expectations of what artificial intelligence can and cannot do.

Algorithmic bias *and ethical issues*: artificial intelligence algorithms can inadvertently introduce bias, leading to ethical issues. Ensuring that artificial intelligence systems are fair and unbiased is a key challenge.

Tools and solutions to address these challenges

Data protection tools: tools such as OneTrust and TrustArc help companies manage data protection and regulatory compliance.

AI integration platforms: platforms such as Zapier and MuleSoft help you integrate AI tools into your existing systems.

Online training platforms: resources such as Coursera and Udemy offer courses to familiarize your team with artificial intelligence and data analytics.

Cost management tools: tools like Allocadia can help you manage the marketing budget and ROI of your AI implementation.

Although the introduction of artificial intelligence into marketing strategy has immense potential, it also presents some challenges. Addressing issues related to data protection, systems integration, skills gaps, cost management, setting expectations, and ethical concerns is critical to successful implementation. With the right tools and approaches, companies can overcome these challenges and harness the full power of artificial intelligence to improve their marketing strategies. As artificial intelligence continues to evolve, adaptability and intelligence will be critical to effectively address these challenges. Embarking on the journey toward integrating artificial intelligence (AI) into marketing is both exciting and challenging. For companies taking their first steps in this direction, it is important to approach AI with a strategic mindset and practical considerations.

Practical tips for getting started with AI in marketing

Understand your needs and goals: Start by understanding what you want to achieve with artificial intelligence in your marketing strategy. Clear goals guide the process of integrating artificial intelligence, such as enhancing the customer experience, improving targeting, and automating repetitive tasks.

Start small and scale up gradually: Don't feel compelled to implement large-scale AI solutions right away. To understand how artificial intelligence works and how it can help your marketing efforts, start with smaller, more manageable projects.

Choose the right AI tool: Choose an AI tool that aligns with your marketing goals and is appropriate for your company's size and industry. Tools such as HubSpot for marketing automation and Google Analytics for data analysis are a good place to start.

Focus on data quality: Artificial intelligence is heavily data- driven, so make sure you have access to relevant, high-quality data. Clean and organize existing data and establish continuous processes for data collection and management.

Make sure your team understands the basics of artificial intelligence and its applications in marketing. Investing in training and development will help your team effectively use artificial intelligence tools and interpret the information they provide.

Performance monitoring and measurement: regularly monitor the performance of your AI initiatives. Measures success and identifies opportunities for improvement using metrics and KPIs.

Stay up-to-date on artificial intelligence trends: The field of artificial intelligence is rapidly evolving. Stay up-to-date on the latest trends and advances in AI technology to ensure that your marketing strategy remains relevant and effective.

Prioritize customer privacy and ethical issues: Consider customer privacy and ethical issues related to artificial intelligence. Ensure compliance with data protection regulations and offer transparency to your customers about the use of their data.

Beginning to use artificial intelligence in marketing requires a thoughtful and strategic approach. Set clear goals, start small, choose the right tools, focus on data quality, educate your team, monitor performance, stay informed, and prioritize ethical considerations. In this way, you can better integrate artificial intelligence into your marketing strategy and maximize its potential. As you become more familiar with artificial intelligence, you can explore more advanced applications and tools to further enhance your marketing efforts. Introducing artificial intelligence (AI) into your marketing strategy is an important step in bringing innovation and efficiency. To ensure a successful implementation of artificial intelligence, it is important to follow best practices that align with your business and marketing goals.

BEST PRACTICES FOR IMPLEMENTATION

Clearly define your goals: First, define what you want to achieve with artificial intelligence. The implementation of artificial intelligence requires clear goals, such as increasing customer loyalty, personalizing marketing campaigns and optimizing advertising spending.

Ensure data quality and accessibility: The quality of an AI system is determined by the data it processes. Make sure you have access to relevant, high-quality data and that your systems can easily access and process that data.

Choosing the right AI solution: Not all AI tools are the same. Choose the AI solution that best fits your specific needs and marketing goals. Tools such as Salesforce. Einstein for customer information and Marketo for marketing automation may be good options.

Integrate artificial intelligence into existing workflows: Artificial intelligence should complement and enhance existing marketing workflows. Make sure artificial intelligence tools are seamlessly integrated into your current systems and processes.

Focus on user experience: Whether it's chatbots or personalized content, the ultimate goal of artificial intelligence should be to improve the user experience. Put customer needs and preferences at the center of your artificial intelligence efforts.

Performance monitoring and measurement: regularly monitor the performance of AI tools . Use analytics to measure the impact on your marketing goals and make necessary changes.

Stay up-to-date on artificial intelligence trends: The field of artificial intelligence is constantly evolving. Stay up-to-date on the latest trends and advances in AI technology to keep your marketing strategies relevant and effective.

Prioritize ethical considerations and compliance: Consider ethical considerations and privacy compliance. Ensure that your implementation of artificial intelligence respects customer privacy and meets legal standards.

The implementation of artificial intelligence in marketing requires a strategic approach and adherence to best practices. Define clear goals, ensure data quality, choose the right tools, integrate artificial intelligence into existing workflows, focus on user experience, monitor performance, stay current on trends and ethical considerations. By prioritizing things, you can effectively integrate artificial intelligence into your business. This approach helps you harness the full potential of artificial intelligence to improve your marketing initiatives and achieve your business goals.

Measuring the ROI of AI strategies in marketing

Measuring the return on investment (ROI) of an artificial intelligence (AI) strategy in marketing is important for understanding its effectiveness and value. It is important to consider how your artificial intelligence-related efforts will help you achieve your business goals and justify your investment in these technologies. To measure ROI, it is important to consider important considerations such as: Define clear metrics: start by defining specific metrics in line with your business goals. This includes increasing sales, increasing engagement rates, improving customer satisfaction, reducing operating costs, and more. Baseline measurement: Measure current performance parameters before implementing artificial intelligence. This foundation will help you evaluate the impact of artificial intelligence on your marketing strategy.

Keep track of incremental improvements: Keep track of improvements made by the AI over time. This includes tracking increased customer loyalty, increased conversion rates, saving time in marketing activities and more.

Cost-benefit analysis: Compare the costs of implementing and maintaining AI solutions with the benefits obtained. This includes direct costs such as software subscriptions and indirect costs such as training and onboarding.

Long-term value assessment: Go beyond the immediate benefits and consider the long-term value brought by artificial intelligence, including the best customer insights to guide future marketing strategies.

Tools for measuring the ROI of AI

Google Analytics: Used to monitor website traffic, user behavior, conversion rates, and evaluate the impact of SEO and content strategy based on artificial intelligence.

HubSpot: Provides artificial intelligence-based analytics to monitor the performance and customer retention of your email marketing campaigns.

Hootsuite Analytics: Helps you measure the effectiveness of your AI-based social media strategies, including engagement and reach.

Measuring the ROI of AI can be difficult because of the complexity of quantifying benefits such as: Improving customer experience and brand awareness can be difficult. In addition, artificial intelligence strategies take time to see tangible results and require patience and long-term vision. Measuring the ROI of an AI strategy in marketing is important to understand its effectiveness and guide future investments. By defining clear metrics, tracking incremental improvements, conducting cost-benefit analyses and using the right tools, companies can effectively measure the ROI of their artificial intelligence initiatives. This approach ensures that your artificial intelligence strategy is aligned with your business goals and contributes to the Overall marketing success. Scaling artificial intelligence (AI) initiatives is also a key step in expanding the impact of AI in different aspects of marketing. It involves moving beyond initial pilot projects to broader implementation, ensuring that AI-based strategies are seamlessly integrated into various marketing activities.

But what are the key steps for scaling AI in marketing?

Identify early successes and insights: Evaluate the results of your early artificial intelligence projects before scaling them back. Identify what went well and what areas need improvement. This review will guide you through the downsizing process.

Create a scalable roadmap for artificial intelligence: Create a strategic plan that outlines how you will integrate artificial intelligence into different areas of marketing over time. This roadmap should be in line with your overall business and marketing goals.

Ensure a robust data infrastructure: As efforts related to artificial intelligence grow, the demand for data will also increase. Make sure your data infrastructure can handle large data sets and more complex analyses.

Integration of artificial intelligence across all channels: Gradually integrate artificial intelligence into marketing channels such as social media, email marketing, and digital advertising to maximize their impact.

Invest in training and development: As artificial intelligence becomes a key part of your marketing strategy, invest in training your team to effectively use artificial intelligence tools and interpret insights.

Choose scalable artificial intelligence tools: Choose scalable artificial intelligence tools and platforms with your business. A flexible and adaptable tool is desirable.

Performance monitoring and iteration: continuously monitor the performance of your AI initiatives and make iterative improvements. This continuous optimization is the key to successful scalability.

Tools for scaling artificial intelligence in marketing

Salesforce Einstein: Offers scalable artificial intelligence solutions for customer relationship management and marketing insights.

Adobe Sensei: Provides artificial intelligence and machine learning capabilities that can be integrated into various Adobe marketing tools.

Marketo: Adobe company, offers marketing automation tools that scale with artificial intelligence integration.

Scaling up artificial intelligence-related efforts can be difficult because integrating artificial intelligence into various marketing functions is complex and requires continuous data analysis and interpretation. In addition, it is important to keep your team prepared and maintain privacy and security. Scaling up artificial intelligence efforts in marketing requires careful planning, a robust data infrastructure, team training, and continuous performance monitoring. By following these steps and leveraging scalable artificial intelligence tools, companies can effectively increase the impact of artificial intelligence in their marketing strategies and promote innovation and efficiency at scale. In the rapidly evolving field of artificial intelligence (AI), it is important for marketers to stay abreast of the latest trends. Staying abreast of new developments ensures that your marketing strategies are always innovative and effective.

THE IMPORTANCE OF KEEPING UP WITH TRENDS IN THE AI

Artificial intelligence technology is constantly advancing, creating new opportunities and challenges for marketing. Staying informed allows you to adapt your strategy, leverage new tools, and gain a competitive advantage.

Follow industry experts and thought leaders: Subscribe to blogs, podcasts, and social media channels of artificial intelligence experts and thought leaders. This provides information on emerging trends and best practices.

Attend conferences and webinars: Attend industry conferences, webinars and workshops on artificial intelligence in marketing. These events are a great way to learn about the latest technologies and network with experts.

Join online communities: Join online forums and communities where marketing and artificial intelligence experts discuss trends, challenges, and solutions. Platforms such as LinkedIn and Reddit groups can be valuable resources.

Subscribe to related publications: Regularly read industry publications and journals focused on artificial intelligence and digital marketing. Publications such as "AI Magazine" and "Marketing AI Institute" provide valuable information.

Leverage AI News Aggregator: Leverage AI News Aggregator to collect the latest news and articles on AI. Tools like Feedly can help you organize and stay informed.

Continuous learning and training: Sign up for an online course or training program focused on artificial intelligence and its applications in marketing. Platforms such as Coursera and Udemy offer courses to keep you up to date.

Experiment with new tools: Be willing to experiment with new artificial intelligence tools and technologies. This hands-on experience will give you practical insight into the benefits of artificial intelligence for your marketing strategy.

The speed at which artificial intelligence is advancing is astonishing. It is important to focus on the trends most relevant to your marketing goals and avoid getting distracted by any new developments. Staying up-to-date on artificial intelligence trends is important for modern marketers. Stay current with your marketing strategy by following industry experts, attending relevant events, interacting with online communities, reading publications, using news aggregators, continuously learning and experimenting with new tools. You can take advantage of advances in artificial intelligence. This proactive approach will help you effectively integrate artificial intelligence into your marketing strategy and stay ahead of the competitive digital marketing landscape.

CHAPTER 5

SOCIAL MEDIA MARKETING: PAST, FUTURE AND APPLICATIONS

The evolution of the Internet from Web 1.0 to Web 3.0 has radically changed social media marketing. This initiative reflects the shift from static websites to interactive and decentralized platforms, changing the way companies and others connect with their audiences.

Web 1.0: Static Internet

Web 1.0, also known as the "read-only" Internet, was the first stage in the development of the World Wide Web. Here the content was static and user interaction was minimal. The website was like a digital brochure with very little user- generated content. For marketers, this era meant having an online presence, but with limited opportunities for engagement and interaction.

The transition to Web 2.0: The Social Web

Web 2.0 marked a major shift toward a more interactive and social Web.

This era introduced platforms such as Facebook, Twitter, and YouTube that enabled users not only to consume content, but also to create and share it. In the Web 2.0 era, social media marketing has changed to engage audiences, build communities and encourage two-way conversations. It was a time when digital marketing was growing significantly and companies were using social media for brand awareness, customer loyalty and targeted advertising.

The emergence of Web 3.0: Decentralized Web

Web 3.0 represents the next phase in the evolution of the Internet, with a focus on decentralization and user sovereignty. It features technologies such as blockchain, artificial intelligence and the Internet of Things (IoT). In Web 3.0, data become more interconnected in the Semantic Web, and artificial intelligence plays a key role in providing personalized experiences for users. The latter opens up new avenues for social media marketing.

Increased personalization: AI-based algorithms can provide highly personalized content and recommendations based on user behavior and preferences.

Blockchain for transparency and trust: Blockchain technology can increase transparency in marketing campaigns and increase trust between brands and consumers.

Using IoT for marketing: IoT devices provide a wealth of data that can be used to understand consumer habits and preferences, enabling more targeted marketing strategies. The evolution from Web 1.0 to Web 3.0 marks a major shift in social media marketing.

From static Web sites to interactive platforms to the decentralized Web based on artificial intelligence, each phase has brought new opportunities and challenges for marketers. Understanding this evolution is important for those who wish to adapt their strategies and take advantage of technology more recent to interact effectively with one's audience.

As we enter the Web 3.0 era, the potential for innovative and effective social media marketing continues to grow. Social media marketing is an ever-evolving field with new trends emerging all the time. It is important for marketers to stay abreast of these trends to remain effective and relevant. Here are some of the latest trends shaping the social media marketing landscape.

1. The rise of short video content

Platforms such as TikTok and Instagram Reels have increased the popularity of short video content. These platforms offer creative and engaging ways to quickly capture your audience's attention. Brands are using short videos for storytelling, product presentation, and user engagement.

2. Influencer marketing continues to grow

Influencer marketing is not a new trend, but it is evolving. Brands are now focused on building long-term relationships with influencers who align with their values. Micro-influencers with small but involved audiences are especially valuable.

3. The increasing use of artificial intelligence and machine learning

Artificial intelligence and machine learning are increasingly being used to analyze consumer behavior, personalize content and optimize advertising campaigns. Tools such as ChatGPT for interactive content generation and Google Analytics for data analysis are becoming essential.

4. Growth of social commerce

Social media platforms are increasingly integrating e-commerce features. Instagram Shopping and Facebook Marketplace are examples that allow users to shop directly from their social media apps, providing a seamless shopping experience.

5. Valuing authenticity and transparency

Consumers expect authenticity and transparency from brands on social media. User-generated content, behind-the-scenes contributions, and honest communication are effective in building trust and loyalty.

6. Focus on social listening

Social listening tools are becoming increasingly important for understanding audience sentiment and trends. Tools such as Brandwatch and Mention provide information about what consumers are saying about your brand online.

7. Sustainability and social responsibility

Consumers are increasingly attracted to brands that demonstrate social responsibility and sustainability. Social media campaigns that highlight your brand's commitment to these values are likely to resonate with your audience.

8. Interactive content

Interactive content such as polls, quizzes, and AR filters will further increase user interest. Platforms such as Snapchat with AR capabilities are being used creatively for marketing campaigns. The social media marketing landscape is dynamic and trends are evolving rapidly.

From short-form video content to influencer marketing, from artificial intelligence integration to social commerce, it is important for marketers to take advantage of these trends to stay ahead of the curve. As social media continues to evolve, staying current and adaptable is key to a successful marketing strategy. Social media marketing will undergo even more fundamental changes in the future. Anticipating these trends helps marketers prepare and adapt their strategies to stay ahead of the curve. Here are some key predictions about the future of social media marketing.

1. Integration of augmented reality (AR) and virtual reality (VR)

The integration of AR and VR into social media is increasing to provide users with immersive experiences. Brands can use AR for virtual testing or virtual reality for immersive product experiences to increase customer loyalty and interactions.

2. Continued growth of video content

Video content, particularly live streaming, is expected to dominate social media. Platforms could introduce more features to support video content, and brands could invest more resources in video production.

3. Advanced personalization with artificial intelligence

Artificial intelligence continues to evolve and enable even higher levels of personalization in social media marketing. This could include the creation of highly personalized, AI-based content based on the preferences and behaviors of individual users.

4. Growth of social commerce

Social commerce is expected to grow as more and more platforms integrate shopping features. The seamless integration of social media and e-commerce offers brands more ways to connect directly with their customers.

5. Growing concern over user privacy and data security

As consumers become more aware of privacy issues, social media platforms and marketers must prioritize data security and transparency in their operations.

6. Expansion of influencer marketing

Influencer marketing can evolve to focus on long-term partnerships and collaborations with influencers who align closely with a brand's values and ethos.

7. Increase in niche social platforms

Niche social platforms that cater to specific interests or communities may be on the rise. Marketers need to identify and target audiences on these specialized platforms.

8. The increasing use of interactive user-generated content

Interactive content, such as polls, quizzes, and user-generated content campaigns, are becoming increasingly popular to stimulate engagement and foster community.

The future of social media marketing will be dynamic and user-centered, with technological advances such as AR/VR, AI, and social commerce playing a key role. Marketers must be agile, embrace new technologies and remain sensitive to consumer concerns about privacy and trust. By anticipating these changes, brands can position themselves to effectively engage their audiences in the evolving social media landscape.

Social Media Marketing and Dropshipping

Dropshipping is a business model in which retailers sell products without inventory and is gaining tremendous momentum in the age of social media. The rise of social media platforms has changed dropshipping, making it more accessible and effective for entrepreneurs and small businesses. When a customer places a dropshipping order, the seller purchases the product from a third party and the third party ships it directly to the customer. This model eliminates the need for inventory management and large upfront investments, making it an attractive option for many. But what role does social media play in dropshipping?

Marketing and customer acquisition: Social media platforms are powerful tools for marketing your dropshipping products. They offer targeted advertising options that allow dropshippers to reach specific target groups with their products.

Brand Building: Social media offers dropshippers an opportunity to build a brand identity. Build a loyal customer base through consistent postings and engagement.

Partnership with influencers: Partnering with influencers on social media increases the visibility and credibility of your dropshipping products and boosts sales.

Customer feedback and engagement: Social media allows direct interaction with customers, provides valuable feedback and fosters a sense of community around your brand.

Tools and platforms for dropshipping in the age of social media Shopify: A popular e-commerce platform that integrates easily with various dropshipping providers and provides tools to set up an online store.

Oberlo: A Shopify app that connects retailers and suppliers and makes it easy to add products to your store.

Facebook and Instagram ads: Powerful tools for targeting potential customers based on interests, behavior and demographic data.

Social media offers many opportunities for dropshipping, but it also brings challenges. These include strong competition, the need for continuous marketing efforts, and maintaining product quality and customer satisfaction. Dropshipping in the age of social media offers entrepreneurs a unique opportunity to start and grow a business with minimal investment. By using social media for marketing, brand building and customer engagement, dropshippers can reach a wide audience and create successful online businesses. However, it is important to address the challenges carefully and continue to adapt to the ever-changing social media landscape.

Leveraging social media for dropshipping success

In the dropshipping world, social media is an invaluable tool for increasing sales and developing brand awareness. With the right strategy, dropshippers can effectively use social media platforms to reach their target audience and grow their business.

Key strategies for using social media with dropshipping

Targeted advertising: Take advantage of the targeted advertising capabilities of social media platforms such as Facebook and Instagram. These platforms allow you to target specific demographic data based on interests, behavior and location, making your ads more effective.

Create engaging content: Create engaging and relevant content that resonates with your audience. This includes product demos, customer testimonials, and lifestyle images that showcase your products in real-life scenarios.

Collaboration with Influencers: Collaborate with influencers who share your brand values and have an audience that follows you. Influencers can provide authentic advice, increasing your reach and credibility. Interactive posts and stories: engage your audience and gather feedback with interactive features such as polls, quizzes, and Q&A sessions in your posts and stories.

Consistent brand message: Maintain a consistent brand voice and aesthetic across all social media channels. This consistency helps build a recognizable and trusted brand.

Loyalty and customer service: Leverage social media platforms to provide responsive customer service and engage your audience.

Build a loyal customer base by responding to comments, posts and reviews. Use user-generated content: Encourage customers to share their experiences with your products. User-generated content serves as powerful social proof and increases brand credibility.

Tools for improving Dropshipping on social media

Canva: Create visually appealing graphics and marketing materials.

Hootsuite or Buffer: To schedule and manage social media posts on various platforms.

BuzzSumo: Analyze which content is most effective in your social media niche.

Social media offers huge opportunities for dropshipping businesses, but it is important to keep platform algorithms up to date, manage ad spend and stand out in a crowded marketplace. Leveraging social media for dropshipping success requires a strategic approach focused on targeted advertising, engaging content, collaboration with influencers, and consistent brand messages. With the right tools and strategies, dropshippers can effectively leverage social media to grow their business, build customer loyalty and build a strong online presence. Dropshipping, while a profitable e-commerce model, presents a number of challenges. Understanding these challenges and implementing effective solutions is critical to running a successful dropshipping business, especially in the context of social media marketing.

Product quality control: Direct shippers do not manage inventory;

therefore, product quality control can be difficult.

Supplier Reliability: Supplier dependence means that any delays or problems on the part of the supplier have a direct impact on the business.

High competition: Dropshipping has a low barrier to entry, making it highly competitive and difficult to stand out from the crowd.

Customer Service: It can be difficult to provide effective customer service when you do not have direct control over shipping and inventory.

Profit margins: Competition, advertising and marketing costs can make it difficult to maintain profit margins.

Solutions to address these challenges Carefully evaluate suppliers: Build strong relationships with trusted suppliers. Use platforms such as AliExpress and SaleHoo to find proven and reliable suppliers.

Focus on niche markets: To reduce competition, focus on niche products or markets. This allows for a more targeted marketing and potentially higher profit margins. Improve customer service: Use customer service tools such as Zendesk and Freshdesk to efficiently handle customer inquiries. Be transparent with your customers about delivery times and policies.

Quality control measures: Order samples of the product to check its quality. Regularly review customer feedback to identify recurring problems.

Using social media for marketing: Effective use of social media platforms for marketing. Engage your audience, use targeted advertising and create engaging content to attract and retain customers.

SEO optimization: invest in SEO for your dropshipping store to increase organic traffic. Tools such as SEMrush and Ahrefs can help you optimize your website.

Automate when possible: Use automation tools to streamline processes such as order processing, inventory management and e-mail marketing.

Dropshipping offers great opportunities for entrepreneurs, but challenges such as product quality, supplier reliability, competition, customer service and profit margins must be carefully managed. By implementing strategic solutions such as supplier selection, focusing on niche markets, improving customer service, and leveraging social media and SEO, dropshippers can overcome these challenges and build successful businesses. Adaptability and customer focus are the keys to success in the dynamic world of dropshipping.

Social Media Marketing and Influencer Marketing

Influencer marketing is a cornerstone of modern social media strategies and is revolutionizing the way brands interact with their audiences. This approach leverages the influence of people with a large following on social media platforms to promote your products and services. Influencer marketing involves working with social media celebrities to gain followers. These influencers have built a level of trust and engagement with their audience, which makes their advice valuable.

Factors contributing to the rise of influencer marketing

Changing consumer trust: Consumer trust is declining with traditional advertising. People tend to trust the advice of people they respect and follow-on social media.

Increased use of social media: Increased use of social media has created fertile ground for influencer marketing. Platforms such as Instagram, YouTube and TikTok have become great places for influencers to connect with their audiences.

Targeted reach: influencers often have a specific niche, which allows brands to reach their target audience more effectively than broadband advertising.

Credibility and relevance: influencers are perceived as more trustworthy and relevant than traditional celebrities, making their endorsements more effective.

Influencer marketing has evolved from simple product mentions to more sophisticated collaborations, including long-term partnerships, co-branding products, and developing influencers into brand ambassadors.

Influencer marketing tools and platforms

AspireIQ: Connect and collaborate with brands and influencers. Provides campaign management and performance monitoring tools.

BuzzSumo: helps you identify influencers in a specific field based on the reach and engagement of their content.

HypeAuditor: provides analysis and insights into influencer audiences, helping brands assess the credibility and effectiveness of potential partners.

Despite its effectiveness, influencer marketing faces challenges such as ensuring credibility, measuring ROI, and managing the complexity of influencer-brand relationships. There is also the risk of influencer scandals affecting a brand's image (recall the recent incident of Barocco Panettone in collaboration with famous influencer Chiara Ferrari). The rise of influencer marketing reflects a major shift in consumer behavior and marketing strategy. It emphasizes the power of authenticity, targeted reach, and social media personalities in shaping consumer preferences. For brands, addressing this situation requires a strategic approach focused on building true partnerships and leveraging the right tools to maximize the impact of influencer collaborations. As social media continues to evolve, influencer marketing will continue to be an important part of an effective digital marketing strategy.

Strategies for effective collaborations with influencers

Collaborating with influencers has become an important strategy in social media marketing. It is important to approach these partnerships strategically to maximize their effectiveness. Here are some key strategies for successful influencer partnerships.

1. Selecting the right influencer

The success of an influencer campaign depends largely on working with the right influencer. Look for influencers who align with your target audience and whose values align with your brand. Tools like BuzzSumo and HypeAuditor can help you identify influencers with the right demographics and audience engagement rates.

2. Focus on authenticity

Authenticity is the key to influencer marketing. Partner with influencers who have a connection or genuine interest in your product or service. Authentic advice is more likely to resonate with your audience and lead to greater engagement.

3. Set clear goals and expectations

Set clear goals for your influencer campaign, including: Increase brand awareness, boost sales or increase followers on social media. Communicate goals and expectations with influencers to ensure alignment and effective collaboration.

4. Encouraging creative freedom

Providing guidelines is important, but giving influencers creative freedom can help them produce more authentic and engaging content. Influencers know their audience best, so rely on their expertise when creating content.

5. Use multiple platforms

Don't limit your collaboration with influencers to one platform. Maximize your reach and influence by using the various social media platforms your target group is active on, such as Instagram, YouTube, TikTok, and Twitter.

6. Building long-term partnerships

Consider building long-term relationships with influencers rather than one-off campaigns. Long-term partnerships can lead to more authentic advertising and better collaboration between brands and influencers.

7. Performance measurement and analysis

Use analytics tools to monitor the performance of your influencer campaigns. Tools such as Google Analytics and AspireIQ provide insights into traffic, engagement and conversion through collaboration with influencers.

8. Stay up-to-date on compliance and regulations.

Ensure that collaborations with influencers comply with legal requirements and social media platform policies, including clear disclosure of sponsored content. Effective influencer collaborations require selecting the right influencer, fostering credibility, setting clear goals, creative freedom, leveraging multiple platforms, engaging in long-term partnerships, and performance. It requires a strategic approach focused on measurement and compliance.

By implementing these strategies, companies can harness the full potential of influencer marketing to improve their social media presence and achieve their marketing goals. In conclusion, measuring the impact of influencer marketing is essential to understanding its effectiveness and guiding future marketing strategies. By focusing on key metrics, leveraging the right tools, setting clear goals and engaging in regular analysis, companies can gain a comprehensive understanding of their influencer marketing efforts. This data-driven approach ensures that influencer marketing remains an integral and effective part of your strategy to social media marketing.

CONCLUSION

In a journey of exploration between the winding path of social media marketing and the surprising developments in intelligence artificial, we examined how these two forces are redefining the landscape of communication and business. By the end of this book, we are faced with an ever-expanding horizon full of unexplored possibilities and urgent challenges. Inextricably linked to further developments in artificial intelligence, the future of social media marketing promises to be not only revolutionary, but also surprisingly human. Although technology is advancing rapidly, people are still at the center of this ecosystem, with their wants, needs and stories. In this context, artificial intelligence is not only a tool for achieving effectiveness and precision, but also a means of understanding humans more deeply and connecting with them in increasingly personal and meaningful ways. Looking ahead, social media marketing will evolve to become more intuitive and interactive, with artificial intelligence expected to be produced not only by analyzing data but also by predicting users' needs and preferences, creating increasingly personalized experiences. This means a change in the nature of marketing. It is a shift from an activity based primarily on communicating a message to one deeply rooted in experiences and relationship building. Another key aspect that emerges is the issue of ethics and accountability. As artificial intelligence becomes increasingly sophisticated, there is an urgent need to address issues of privacy, transparency, and ethical use of data. These are not just technical details, but issues that go to the heart of trust between brands and consumers. In an increasingly data-driven world, maintaining the balance between personalization and privacy is one of the most delicate and important challenges.

In summary, the future of social media marketing enabled by artificial intelligence takes us into exciting and uncharted territory. It will be a path that requires not only technological innovation, but also a deep ethical commitment and an ever- deepening understanding of human nature. The possibilities are endless, but it is our collective wisdom that will determine the direction and quality of our journey into the future. Looking to the future, it is important to recognize that the integration of social media marketing and artificial intelligence is not only a matter of technological progress, but also of cultural and social development. Companies that successfully navigate these waters will not only embrace cutting-edge technologies, but will also understand and respect the human dynamics behind social media. In this new landscape, it is important for companies to develop the ability not only to listen to their audiences, but to truly interact with them. In this sense, artificial intelligence becomes a powerful ally in analyzing and interpreting human language and emotions, enabling deeper and more meaningful engagement. But we must remember that technology is a tool and must be guided by deep human understanding and empathy. In addition, the democratization of access to artificial intelligence opens up new perspectives in the field of marketing. This will no longer be the exclusive domain of large companies with significant resources, but will also be accessible to small and medium-sized enterprises, redefining the concepts of competitiveness and innovation. This leveling of the playing field is expected to stimulate an unprecedented diversity of opinions and ideas in the market, enriching the digital marketing ecosystem. Advances in artificial intelligence and social media marketing also bring with them the responsibility to train a new generation of professionals. In addition to providing the necessary technical skills, it is also important to develop an ethical and critical understanding of the broader implications of these technologies. Continuing education and training will ensure that future generations of marketing professionals are not only technology savvy, but also aware of their role in shaping an increasingly connected and data-driven society. Ultimately, the convergence of social media marketing and artificial intelligence challenges us to consider what it means to be human in the digital age. In a world where the boundaries between real and virtual are increasingly blurred, our humanity with its imperfections, emotions and connections remains the beacon that guides all innovation. This book has explored the extraordinary possibilities that open up at the intersection of these two powerful forces, but the most exciting chapters have yet to be written. And we all write by choice, for our creativity, but mostly for our humanity.